gonna
finish
that
dragon?

Barry Parham

ALSO BY BARRY PARHAM

Why I Hate Straws
An offbeat worldview of an offbeat world

Sorry, We Can't Use Funny

Blush
Politics and other unnatural acts

The Middle-Age of Aquarius

Full Frontal Stupidity

Chariots of Ire

You Gonna

Finish

That Dragon?

(musings from a table for one)

BARRY PARHAM

ISBN: 14905-56737
ISBN-13: 978-14-9055-6734

The Menu.

DEDICATION

This book is dedicated to Chinese food.
And to Marco Polo.

In a world where everything American is made in China -
even American flags - Chinese food may be the only
product from China that's actually made in America.

And Marco Polo? He delivered Chinese food
to my ancestors.

Marco Polo invented Chinese take-out.

Thanks, Marco.
A whole lot of single guys appreciate it.

Introduction

So.

Here we are: my tenth book, if you count the seven I actually wrote and the three I made up while writing this sentence. This book is the other half of my bold, conceptual two-book trilogy, *It's, like, America and Stuff.*

If you've made it this far in the book, you've seen the cover; the dedication; the table of contents...and depending on your expectations, you're either excited to dive in to a book about food, or you're hoping there's been some mistake. (Of course, after you finish the book, you still might think there's been some mistake.)

Within these pages, we'll discuss globally-significant topics - many of them true - topics such as books you can finish before the Mayan Apocalypse, what all the tony trend-setters will be wearing on National Mule Day, and the shocking connection between the ancient Olympics, Joe Biden's teeth, and Paul Revere's horse.

Really.

For Starters

~*~*~

"Schizophrenia: it beats dining alone."

Oscar Levant

"Hell is other people at breakfast."

Jean-Paul Sartre

~*~*~*~*~

Barry Parham

May I Have This Danse Macabre?

That's okay. Keep the ring. No, really.

<>~<>~~~~~~~~~<>~<>~~~~~~~~~~<>~<>

Not long ago, I had a brief mental lapse. Or I hit my head. Whatever the cause, the result was I started thinking about dating again. Maybe. Probably not, but maybe.

But three things I saw in the news caused me to can *that* idea.

1) a woman with well-kept skin shot her boyfriend
2) *...and* stabbed him 27 times
3) *...and* forgot she did it

Aaaaand ... boom. End of urge. Lapse over.

See, in the fairly simple cause-and-effect world of a Single Guy, when the lady you're currently seeing kills you twenty-eight times, this is what's known as a *'CLUE.'*

Basically, the motivation behind most Single Guy Decisions can be summed up in two words: low maintenance. Single guys can go through an entire week and never have thoughts any more complicated than these two:

1) Cute girl. Wonder what she's like?
2) Can I eat this?

Occasionally, the second question may be amended to become "Can I eat this and not die?" - depending on the color of the food in question, and how far back in the fridge it was when you found it. (Single guys are unsung experts at classifying the age and toxicity of potentially edible stuff, based on the stuff's position, relative to other stuff on the shelf. We call it "lateral archaeology.")

But sensibly qualifying the question "Can I eat this?" is one thing. It's another thing entirely having to work forensics into the first question: "Cute girl. Wonder if she'll kill me?"

No matter how you define it, "low maintenance" ends where "running for your life" begins.

Plus, I hate it when women start comparing you to their ex-beaus. "Oh, move it along, would ya? Sheesh. My last three boyfriends bled out in 20 minutes. *Tops.*"

The news story that dialed back my dating dilemma? Yet more courtroom coverage of yet another 'crimes of passion' trial, this one involving a former blonde and an eventually former guy.

It's a story we've seen many times before: boy meets girl; girl blacks out; boy dies of natural causes resulting from an unholy abundance of Republican assault weapons (and from leaping in front of a knife 27 times); girl dyes hair, dons glasses, pleads 'not guilty;' lawyer defends girl's innocence, citing tough childhood (hers, not his); girl writes tell-all book; lawyer negotiates for movie rights (his, not hers); lawyer dumps girl; girl slays again; film at eleven.

I'm sure you know, or know *of,* the trial, because it's one of those unfortunately ubiquitous court cases that reporters mention every time they need some filler in-between the 'real' news...

~-~-~-~-~-~

"According to our sources, Joe Biden has just cursed again. That's the third time today the Vice President has sworn out loud, during his speech here at the nunnery. While we wait for his next adjective, let's get an update on that murder trial."

~-~-~-~-~-~

"This is Blitz Wolfer, reporting for Sea & Inn. As global thermonuclear war breaks out here in Pying-Pyong, North Korea, I'm monitoring events with basketball superstar John Kerry and Secretary of State Dennis Rodman. Dennis, by my count, that was the seventeenth consecutive North Korean military rocket to fall over on its side during launch, wouldn't you say? John, your thoughts? Okay, while we wait for John to count to seventeen, let's turn to Cooperson Anders for some unbelievably biased reporting on that murder trial."

~-~-~-~-~-~

"Folks, this is Tab Colander, reporting from Martha's Vineyard. In light of the breaking nuclear holocaust news from North Korea, it looks as if America's chief executive has reached a decision: it's cherry. President Obama has decided to go with the cherry sno-cone."

~-~-~-~-~-~-~

"Welcome to *Today!* We've got a great show for this morning, including an update on that breaking sno-cone situation on the Cape. I'm your host, Katie Couri...no, wait, I'm your host, Meredith Viera...hold on, now it's Matt Lauer...wait, now it's Ann Curry...I'm Kathie Lee Philbin; I mean, Regis Gifford; I mean, Kathie Le...wait, it's me, Matt, again...hi, I'm Hoda Kotb, spelled the way it's usually spelled, and we'll be right back after thi..."

~-~-~-~-~-~-~

Looking back, it was a timeless princess-meets-prince kind of story, with a magical fairy-tale ending, particularly if you were the magical ending's court-appointed lawyer, getting paid $250 an hour by taxpayers to defend the princess.

(Speaking of fairy tales, one 'expert' was paid $250 an hour to interview the perp princess - for 44 hours - and then paid an *additional* $300 an hour to describe the interview in court. Whoa. This story's got more fairy tales than the *NBC Nightly News*, and more happy endings than Bill Gates' pre-nup.)

According to court transcripts, which we're making up as you read this, the trouble started during a visit, one evening, a few weeks after the defendantrix and her ex-boyfriend had agreed to start co-hating each other. For a while, everything went smoothly. They spent the first part of the evening playing a nice, friendly game involving a shower, a camera, and various aerobic forms of interpretive dance.

But at some point, Exhibit A delivered 27 doses of bad juju to Exhibit B, as often happens when people start dating other people without first investing in comprehensive financial and psychological background checks. And sodium pentothal.

Here's a brief timeline of the story's sigh-inspiring highlights:

- The princess meets the prince at the most romantic location imaginable: a Prepaid Legal Services conference in Vegas.
- The prince and princess fall madly in heat.
- Following her new boyfriend's lead, the princess converts to the Church of Latter-Day Saints, a group known for their uncanny ability to attract paralegals who get paid upfront.
- 180 Latter-Days later, the star-crossed pair of paralegals break up.
- Some time later, the prepaid princess borrows two 5-gallon gas cans from one of her rare, surviving ex-princes. According to the borrowee, she offers no explanation. Understandably, the non-perforated ex-boyfriend didn't press.
- Credit card records show that the princess then bought a third gas can.
- ...and facial cleanser.
- ...and some sunblock.

7

- Nobody can shed any light on this weird shopping list, but this is a good time to offer an observation:
- *CLUE!!!*
- Suddenly, the prince turns up dead, or as President Obama might put it, "less than optimal." On the bright side, though: now that he's dead, he's eligible to vote in Chicago.
- Next morning, the *Today!* show does a segment on Republican voter suppression. And facial cleansers.
- Hauled in for questioning, the princess claims amnesia. Detectives note that she exudes a pungent petrol-like aroma, but her pores are fabulous.

Being Quiet

If I'd been born a panther, there'd be a lot more pigs
<>~<>~~~~~~~~~~<>~<>~~~~~~~~~~<>~<>

Let me ask you a question. If a single guy is an overnight guest at a friend's house, and the next morning he tried really hard not to make any noise, would he still sound like a tree fell down in the forest?

I don't know if it's just me, or if it's some kind of cosmic-level Loki-spawned joke, but either way, it's true: you never realize just how noisy you are till you try not to be noisy.

And this past weekend, I discovered that truth yet again.

Over the last few years, if occasionally you've looked in on me and my weekly lapses into literature, you've noticed by now that I'm a simple, stay-at-home guy. Almost everything about me is simple: simple needs (*some music, some food, some more music*); simple concepts in personal fashion (*"All right, I'll wear shoes, but let's not make this a habit"*); simple tastes in politicians (*they should be honest, and terminally ill*).

9

Just a simple guy. I don't expect others to like what I like. I don't butt heads with buttheads; I don't argue for the sake of ego; I don't care for confrontation. I don't even like those annoying "Are you sure?" decision confirmation prompts in computer programs, especially when the decision I'm making is no more dire than deleting yet another marketing email, from some unknown someone, who wants to make sure I've considered the benefits of not waiting till the last second to purchase a casket.

Also, as a single guy who's been single guy-ing it for a long time, I'm a bit of a slave to habit. Okay, that's a bit of an understatement. When it comes to who's in charge - habit or me - I'm pretty much ancient Israel, and habit is Egypt. The truth is, I tend to adjust my routines about as often as water adds another oxygen molecule. I'm a fan of sudden lifestyle change, in the same sense that gravity is a "suggestion" of nature.

Of course, one potential downside of this self-imposed solitary definement is this: in my familiar environment, I'm only moderately clumsy, but whenever I venture beyond my own moat, I tend to become ... let's see ... how can I put it ... I'm about as graceful as Barney Frank during day three of a prison volleyball tournament.

So, last weekend, when I'd accepted a friend's invitation to weekend at the lake, I packed a light (but honest and self-aware) overnight bag:

- extra iPod batteries
- shirts, shorts, splints

- quick-acting clotting medication

For me, spending the night in somebody else's house is just not a common exercise. This is equivalent to crossing an unfriendly border; I'm invading Asgard, the land of Loki, but with insufficient body armor. This is *terra incognita* (a Viking term meaning "*oh, the things I'm gonna do to those shins.*")

I had no illusions about the lake weekend. None. I'd resigned to limping home at weekend's end with *at least* the usual injuries, the kind of wounds I regularly unleash upon myself - during a *normal* evening at home - just from trying to walk across a room furnished with anything more angular than a beanbag cushion.

And remember: this is me *at home* ... this is me in an ecosystem of my own design: one in which *I know where everything is*. Imagine me trying to navigate a minefield filled with somebody *else's* sadistically-positioned stools, stairs, pets, guests, and light switches.

I know me. It's just a matter of time before I get distracted and walk smack into a stove, bark a calf on a cabinet, or forget to notice an exterior wall.

And that's in *daylight*.

It was in the early, pre-dawn furniture gauntlet of Sunday when things *really* got stupid. That's when Loki showed up, leading his little legion of accidental noise amplifiers.

11

It was very early. It was very dark. All I wanted to do was wash my face, brush my teeth, and pad like a panther to the kitchen and its glorious coffee machine. And I'd hope to pull this off without disturbing the hosts, or the guests, or any on-hand Nordic gods of mischief who, as it turns out, can be very vindictive and petty when robbed of their early Sunday beauty sleep by something that looks vaguely panther-shaped, assuming panthers get middle-aged, avoid the gym, and are overly fond of burritos.

First - before even getting out of the bed - I hit my head. But that's okay - I do *that* at home. What was different, on that early Sunday, was the sound my head made after playing Cage Match Wrestling with the bedpost.

I suppose it seemed louder because I was trying to be quiet. But it was a thick, booming, resonant noise, the kind you associate with large continents collapsing, or Chris Christie eating a panther burrito.

I was worried my hosts and their guests heard it. Then I was worried they hadn't ... cause if they hadn't heard *that* racket, then they'd all died in their sleep, which meant I was going to get stuck doing all the laundry.

But Loki wasn't done with me yet.

- In the bathroom, I miscalculated my grip on the faucet and banged my knuckle into the mirror. It was a sound straight from Sea Hunt. They had to have heard it on the space station.

- I didn't want to use the only visible hand towel to mop up the blood, so I leaned over the loo and reached for a decorative tissue dispenser. I spun the standard-issue white roll and prepared to tear off a few squares. But, no: Loki flicked a well-used Mischief switch on his Console of Evil, the decorative dispenser sailed off its wall mount and clattered across the tile, bouncing approximately 643,217 times before spelunking into the floor's brass-fitted HVAC duct.
- After wiping down the vanity, I leaned back to the loo and gingerly flushed the evidence. The toilet gargled and carped like Hillary Clinton giving birth to a Republican Wookie.

Finally, I achieved Camp Coffee Pot, primed and armed it, and carried my bags out to my car. Almost done. I soaked up a few seconds' view of the mirrory, mist-licked lake, and reached for the door of my host's house, beyond ready for that hot cupful.

~-~-~-~-~-~

I'd locked myself out.

~-~-~-~-~-~

But I will have to admit: it's nothing less than a gift: getting to wake up, in a house set on a sheet-of-glass lake, and watch the sun pull itself up and over the South Carolina mountains.

I could definitely live here. If I can get pizza delivered.

And plasma.

Barry Parham

A Guy's Guide to Public Privacy

Hmm...I wonder if the Spanish Inquisition invented
fruitcake?

<>~<>~~~~~~~~~~<>~<>~~~~~~~~~~<>~<>

I was attending a Christmas chorale concert when a friend suggested I write a column about bathrooms. I realize that's not exactly a glowing endorsement of my skills as a humorist, or, for that matter, a glowing endorsement of my friends' confidence in my scribbling skills.

Come to think of it, I guess it doesn't say much for the concert, either.

But it is the holiday season in America, which means guys have to turn off the TV and go places. And in such uncharted places, public bathrooms play an integral, underrated role. All over the country, guys are being forced to put on (preferably matching) socks, swipe their hair into obedience, and leave the house - *often, during a ball game* - to go out and attend various seasonal social functions.

You know what happens next. At these various functions, various hosts will callously carpet-bomb you with 800 gallons

15

of an off-white substance, cleverly marketed under the unassuming alias "eggnog." Eggnog is a digestive-system-disrupting paste first created by the Spanish Inquisition for use on particularly stubborn interviewees. ("Nog" is an ancient Latin term meaning "renal express lane.")

What's worse, the 800 gallons are dolloped at you in 20-micron increments, served in overfilled elfin plastic tumblers etched with holly leaves, snowflakes and exclamation points, and presented on a useless square napkinlet the size of a Congressman's conscience, but cleaner.

Alternatively...or, if your karma *really* stinks, alternately...the inviters will insist that you try a nice goblet (or two, or six) of this year's wine from their Uncle Cletus' private label, Chateau Boxing. ("it's a pesky yet haunting little grape-toned diuretic that we like to call *Chenin Blanc itty Blanc Blanc*.")

And after an hour or so of that, there you are - a helpless, clueless, nog-mustached guy, facing a multiple-front volley of festive fluids. And all advice to the contrary, you forgot to "go" before you left home. Plus, you're wearing uncomfortable clothes and, theoretically, matching socks. Against such an onslaught, a guy and his plumbing don't stand a chance.

So the guy does what he must. He heeds the siren's call. He's just a guy.

The public bathroom is, I think, the only remaining American institution that's not yet been attacked by gender rights activists. (Excluding, of course, the West Coast. At last count, San Francisco had eleven distinct genders, and this weekend they're interviewing two more.) As a result, many of you have never been inside that odd, echoey, decidedly non-aromatic chamber known as the *"men's room."*

And even those of us who qualify for entry *genetically* (or, in San Francisco, *eventually*) are often socially unprepared for the experience.

So, as a public service, let's review some rules of etiquette concerning the room simply labeled "Men."

~-~-~-~-~-~

If you enter a public bathroom and, instead of seeing individual stations along the "wall," you notice a long trough, you should:

A) Move to either end of the trough
B) Run back and forth, shouting "Take *that*, commie! Ack-ack-ack!"
C) Sincerely hope you're in a football stadium

Sometimes in the men's room, there's a line of people waiting. While in line, you should:

A) Return your phone messages
B) Pull out a deck of cards
C) Try to organize a sing-along

Just inside the door of many public bathrooms, there is some kind of fold-up table. What's that for?

A) Those occasional social situations that call for an impromptu human sacrifice

B) An fold-out berth for narcoleptics to grab forty winks, if they're very short narcoleptics (*"Well, officer, the sign did say 'rest room,' didn't it?"*)

C) It's used for changing a baby's diaper, but it has never been used by a guy in the history of there being the possibility of more than one guy in the bathroom at the same time.

When standing next to another guy at the "wall," you should never make:

A) Chit-chat

B) Eye contact

C) A cardigan

However, if you know the next guy, you may feel the need to communicate. Which greeting is most appropriate?

A) Evening, Tom. Whoa! What's in that eggnog? WD-40?

B) Hey, Tom! Glad I caught you. Have you ever considered the variable-length benefits of term life insurance?

C) Tom, I killed again today.

On the other hand, if the next guy at the wall is a stranger to you, avoid the following phrases:

A) My! Aren't *you* tall!

B) These are way nicer than they got at the asylum.

C) Got a minute?

You Gonna Finish That Dragon?

While washing up at the sink, if you happen to make eye contact in the mirror, you should:

A) Nod curtly, then look away and start humming the Marine Corps anthem

B) Mutter something non-committal and guy-like, like "how 'bout those Yankees!" or "Be honest - do I look bloated?"

C) Use your finger to write *"I'm watching you"* on the mirror

~-~-~-~-~-~

One more thing, guys. Remember this: eventually, inevitably, at some point in your life, you will commit the ultimate public facilities faux pas: you will get confused and walk into the Women's Room. When this happens, keep your wits about you, because you have options:

A) Mumble an apology and immediately make your retreat

B) Make some idiot comment like "Hey! Where's the wall? What's with all the stalls? What, are you guys voting?"

C) Memorize everyone's shoes. Later, while mingling at the party, try to find the shoes' owners and strike up a conversation.

I will recommend, however, that you steer clear of any female you see at a holiday party if she's wearing Viet Cong combat boots, or eight-inch stilettos and a leopard-motif leotard with iron ring inserts. Believe me, it's just not worth the effort.

Don't ask.

Barry Parham

The Continuing Adventures of What's-His-Name Boy

Looking for a career change? Keep looking!

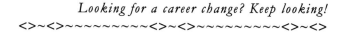

Hey, guys! Ready for a little good news in this numb economy? I think I've found the perfect gig - if you're the right guy. All it requires is low expectations. And a touch of altruism.

And a little spandex.

Now, since I mentioned job requirements like low self-esteem, no recognition, and stretch tights, I know what you guys are thinking: you're thinking, "Hey, I can get treated like that at my *current* job; plus, I don't have to relocate."

You're right. And it's partly my fault. I walked into the discussion; I brought up soul-slaying workweeks, sorry prospects, and Speedos. So naturally you're hoping I've led you out of the wilderness, and put you on the path to pluck a career plum like one of these dream jobs:

- Stand-in actor for an off-season Gilbert & Sullivan festival in south Georgia
- A national security position as Joe Biden's stunt double
- Teaching Assistant who spends his life standing next to a flip chart waiting for somebody to say, "Next, please."

But no - this job offer's a bit different. Here's the scoop:

There's a guy on Craig's List looking for a superhero sidekick.

For those of you who still participate in eighteenth-century activities, like reading books or going outside, Craig's List is an online Classified Ads service, where people like you, me, and Rasputin the mad monk can announce they want to sell something, or buy something, or do something to something during something, while dressed as something and using or chanting something, and to do that something with like-minded people, though we're not ruling out animals, hearth deities, or entirely different species.

Every month, according to the internet, people post somewhere north of sixty million new classified ads at Craig's List, of which at least eleven have been spellchecked. In support of those sixty million posts, Craig's List admits to funding a staff of about thirty people, a clerk-to-customer ratio approximately the same as is found in your average Department of Motor Vehicles.

Personally, I've never used Craig's List, but I did spend nearly five minutes researching it, because when it comes to journalistic integrity, that's the kind of demanding feral animal I am. In a nutshell, Craig's List is like that other online mart, eBay, but without all those pesky, time-consuming design details...you know: color, graphics, page layout, navigation, spell-checking, etc. Spending time at Craig's List is like going out on a dinner date, but without all the bother of putting on clean clothes, or bathing.

And, given that Craig's List is letting a bona fide superhero advertise for a sidekick, the submission guidelines appear to be fairly generous, too.

In his "Sidekick Wanted" ad, the superhero chose to remain anonymous, possibly due to having a secret identity, or a statute of limitations. But he did admit that he's focusing his crime-fighting efforts on the city of Atlanta, which is kind of silly, because there are no people left in Atlanta to commit any crimes. Atlanta, in case you haven't tried to drive through (or around) it lately, is Earth's first metropolis populated entirely by cars, trains, and planes. Seventeen trillion vehicles, all just endlessly driving around three unholy, inbred interstates, occasionally exiting onto one of 400,000 streets, all named 'Peachtree.'

The ad begins like this: "I am looking for a Sidekick that will help me fight crime around the city."

There it is. Not a hint of sarcasm, no whining, no hubris ... just another overworked guy in a costume, looking for a boy wonder, and the faster I move away from *that* joke, the better.

Captain Nameless continues:

Applicants should be skilled in any of the following:
- Kung Fu / Karate / Taekwondo
- Hapkido
- Wing Chun
- Wrestling or WWF
- Savate
- Capoeira
- Brazilian Jiu-jitsu

Note the interesting distinction between 'wrestling' and 'World Wrestling Federation.' You gotta admire a purist. I mean, c'mon - there's wrestling, and then there's TV wrestling. I'd say more, but I don't remember how to spell 'wrasslin.'

(To be fair - when our superhero mentioned the WWF, he might have been referring to the World Wildlife Fund. For all I know, there's a huge market in Atlanta for cage-match tag-team panda mud wrestling.)

It seems that, at this point, Captain Neo was beginning to grow a bit desperate for job requirements. For instance, Capoeira is a Brazilian martial art that combines elements of dance and music (music provided by that rave 80s band, Wing Chun, famous for their neo-Hebrew hit, *'Dan Saul Days'*). I guess that's where the spandex comes in ... kind of a cultural cross between *'West Side Story'* and *'Omen XII: Damien Goes to Congress.'* Hapkido, as best as I can tell, is the name of a Korean mid-sized sedan, while Savate is a type of mulled wine, popular among middle-aged white guys who sell vinyl siding insurance and vacation in Tijuana.)

But the Human Shield *is* prepared to compromise. If his Trusty Sidekick applicants prove to be short-timers in the primary sidekick skillsets, they might still qualify via their expertise in weaponry such as:

- Fencing / Archery
- Kendo / Jukendo
- Sword fighting
- Crowbar

Yes, he did. Yes, he said 'crowbar.' (see *'statute of limitations'*)

And now for the tricky bit - the hands-on experience:

Also Please have up to 3 years of experience in

- Warrior Battle
- FBI / CIA / Military
- Ninja / Samarai
- Footclan
- Shadowloo
- Monk
- Police / SWAT
- etc.

Can't you just hear that conversation?

Superhero: So, tell me more about your work as a monk.
Candidate: Are you interested more in the part where I butchered Oriental civilians, or the chanting, celibate part?
Superhero: Either way. What the hey, it's Friday.

Candidate: Actually, I mostly spent my time darning stretch tights.

Superhero: Fair enough. How's your etc.?

According to the internet, by the way, *'Footclan'* is misspelled. But I suppose that's a niggling criticism for me to make, given that the correctly-spelled *'Foot Clan'* is nothing more than a fictional martial arts horde in the fictional Teenage Mutant Ninja Turtles universe.

In case you're not a steady consumer of cartoons featuring non-existent reptiles that run around exhibiting Far Eastern military tactics, the Foot Clan are the main antagonists of the Mutant Ninja Turtles (which means there are others). The Foot Clan are usually led by The Shredder (which means there are others). But what if The Shredder wants a long weekend? Maybe The Shredder should advertise on Craig's List.

So, heads up, candidates! To make an impression in a your average super-sidekick interview, what you really need is to fake three years' experience fighting make-believe cartoon animals, with an imaginary army, on a planet that doesn't exist.

Might be easier to just get a job in civil service.

But what about the run-of-the-mill interview stuff? What about those standard, American superhero job-posting must-haves? You know the list:

- Candidate will have a good work ethic
- Fights crime as a team, or in an unsupervised environment
- Consistently defeats evil on time and under budget

- The ideal candidate will respond professionally to cross-departmental responsibilities, shifting deadlines, and exposure to kryptonite
- Proficiency with Microsoft Office

Now for the bad news. As I mentioned at the beginning, making the world safe from evildoers doesn't pay very well (at least not in Atlanta). And somebody's gotta pay for all those tights. Also sprach Captain Lonely:

Compensation: Gratitude and self-accomplishment is the only form of payment.

So, if you're in it for the money, get out of it. Go find another career, or stick with the one you're on. Sure, self-accomplishment is a nice thing ... when you're six. But later, when you're all growed up and, of an evening, you try to fund your Chinese carry-out by swiping self-accomplishment instead of a bank card, it's gonna be a long, cold, no-shrimp-fried-rice evening.

Finally, just for kicks, I checked out a few more Craig's List listings. And when it comes to good prospects in bad times, it looks like Atlanta is the place to be. Witness:

An Atlanta-based chap at Craig's List is looking to hire 'escorts.' Candidates should send bikini and nude photos, contact #, and a list of any 'limitations.' Candidates should be sexy, curvy and have a 'good work ethic.'

No mention of any specific Microsoft Office skills.

Ol' 55

Some thoughts on growing old gracefully. Or not.

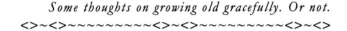

This week, I hit a milesto...strike that.

This week, a milestone hit me. This week, I turned fifty-five.

Fifty-five. I am a speed limit.

I know, I know. Lots of adults pooh-pooh adult birthdays. After all, they say, we're not children anymore. Birthdays are for children only. Children, we're told, should be seen and not heard, whereas adults, I'm told, should be obscene and not absurd. Although I could've misread that.

So grown-ups will employ that irritating, all-knowing cant of the head, purse their lips and stare mistily over your shoulder, and assume that tweed-jacket-with-elbow-patches look that means 'I'm about to impart wisdom all up in here.' Then they'll say things like "oh, I quit counting birthdays" and "after a certain age, birthdays don't matter anymore." You should know a couple of things about these people:

- They're old.
- They're lying.

I think it's fine for adults to celebrate, or at least acknowledge, one's birthday...within reason. I mean, you have to make *some* allowances for being a grown-up. When you're fifty-five, you can just run up to total strangers in restaurants, hold up your fingers, and yell "I'm this many!" Be fair. While you're working out all the 55-year-10-finger schematic issues, their bisque's getting cold.

True: you might get away with such behavior at a Chuck E. Cheese. But if you're celebrating your fifty-plus birthday at Chuck E. Cheese, well ... as Joe Biden might put it: I got three words for you - deep therapy.

And once you get past a certain age, forget about inviting a bunch of friends over to spend the night. That's just not going to end well; plus, it could come back to haunt you if you ever decide to enter the ministry, or run for public office. (Once you're *in* public office, however, sleepovers are practically expected.)

In America, your age is everybody's business. For over four decades now, marketing companies have been asking me what age group I'm in. This is a critical piece of data for marketers, something they call 'demographics' (literal translation: 'number of active credit cards'). And now, I've graduated from the *'45 to 54'* age group to the next one - the penultimate one - the *'55 and Over'* group. (literal translation: 'He's still breathing, or what? Hold a mirror in front of his mouth. Or an active credit card.')

So at fifty-five, I expect to see a whole new onslaught of targeted, tempting, pre-geriatric offers, not to mention a full-on frontal assault by the membership department at AARP (literal translation: 'the Borg collective from *Star Trek*, but with walkers'). That never-resting gang of mercenary marketers has been relentlessly hammering me since I was about eight, possibly because they misinterpreted my age group after I used a compound noun. (literal translation: 'something found in a prison yard')

Month in, month out, with military precision, AARP mails me a thick welcome kit, complete with personalized membership card and several thousand exclamation points. This has been going on since, roughly, the year America landed on the moon, an event which so confused our planet that Billy Preston became the fifth Beatle. (Shortly thereafter, the Beatles broke up, but that was George Bush's fault.)

But the relentless 'Geezer Nation' ad assault from AARP is just one wave in the endless battle for my budget. I have achieved the age when the (e)mailbox fills with very conflicted marketing messages; the Captains of Commerce are sending me some seriously mixed signals. For example, in any given week, I'll get such disjointed "who are they talking to?" calls to action as these:

- Why I should diversify my portfolio with gold
- Why I should abandon all hope and dump my mortgage
- Econo-sized 5-gallon tubs of once-a-day Viagra tablets (*discreetly delivered*)

- 'Don't put if off!' discounts from our tasteful selection of customized caskets *(featuring our bestselling model, the Eterno-Wrap! Now available in your choice of irrelevant colors!)*
- Fabulous lake-front property beginning at only $750,000
- Fabulous penny-pinching weekly bargains on canned meat

If they must mix their messages, couldn't they at least try to be helpful? For example, to brighten up the casket spiel, why not borrow from the Viagra ad?

'Eterno-Wrap is intended for the treatment of Erect Dysfunction, also known as extended horizontality, or persistent deadness. Discuss your status with your doctor to ensure that you are healthy enough for death. Do not stay in this box if you maintain a pulse lasting for more than four hours. Side-effects of not being consistently alive may include a sudden decrease in vision (not to mention heartbeat), chronic tardiness, and a tendency for people to say, "aw, don't he look natural." In some cases, you may be mistaken for comedian Stephen Wright or suddenly find yourself eligible to vote.'

And here's some free medical advice from an on-the-cusp geezer: if, while you're dead, you experience any nausea or sexual discomfort, please contact your physician immediately.

And then, by all means, contact the nearest network television executive.

The Other Hunger Games

I love you. Now pass the hot sauce.

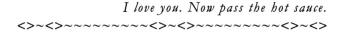

Anybody out there wanna get married?

Now, hold on...before everybody starts running for the exits, please understand - I don't want anything, or expect anything, or want you to expect anything, or anything.

I'm just tired of throwing away all this food.

So don't scoff off my offer just yet, singlettes. Here, in the age of pre-nup regs and post-nup reneges, my idea of a meal-based matrimony might be right up your alley. For a start, here's a list of things you *won't* have to do, or worry about, or put up with:

- Naming the children: First of all, we don't have any. Secondly, we're not likely to have any, because we've gotta finish this food. And thirdly: I've always had a plan, if I ever had a son, to name him 'Gage.' But then Stephen King wrote *Pet Sematary*. In that book, as you know, not only did Mr. King create a kid named 'Gage' - he killed the kid. Horribly. Twice. Thanks, Stephen.

- Giving up your own last name: Not a requirement, not even a my-name-hyphen-your-name compromise. We're splitting *lunch*, not *land*. Plus, I already blew my public school hyphen allotment on all the possible permutations of albums by Crosby & Stills & Nash & Young.

- Weddings: We're not even gonna *discuss* this one. Did you know that the average American wedding now costs somewhere north of $25,000? And that's not counting the cost of the divorce. In fact, according to one recent survey, it costs the average wedding *guest* $539 just to *attend* a wedding! (source: Cheapskate Wedding Guest Trackers, Inc. - a division of Shallow Unlimited)

- Sex: No thanks...not after reading *Pet Sematary*. And after all, this isn't really a marriage, technically speaking, so let's not get all bogged down by social mores and religious restrictions. Ours is just an arrangement of convenience. No reason to drag damnation into it.

So I just thought, maybe, I could find some even-headed reader to even up the odds: you know, you and me, eye-to-eye equals on an extended date, food foot-soldiers against an onslaught of "best if used by" dates.

You Gonna Finish That Dragon?

A single guy wastes a lot of groceries. And I don't mean just the mistakes - the things you shouldn't have bought in the first place (*from freezer to table in twenty seconds!*) - the stuff you toss out due to disappointment, or downright fear. At one time or another, every single guy has bought something like that: although the picture on the package looked exactly like one of your Mom's slow-cooked, entrée-and-all-sides Sunday dinners, the actual results looked more like a genome miscalculation on Dr. Moreau's island.

Ever watched one of those "slit & heat" things heat up in the microwave? Maybe it's just me, but I don't think lunch should throb.

No, the waste I'm talking about is simple volume-based waste. In my opinion, this is a major flaw in the design of grocery stores: it doesn't matter if you're a family of eight or eighteen, a centenarian couple, or a single guy with an unholy attraction to tacos - at the grocery, *everybody* has to buy the same quantities.

To be fair, you *can* buy single servings of food, if you know where to shop. Usually, these single-serving merchants operate little mini-groceries known as 'boutiques.' (literal translation: *ha ha ha ha ha*). Here's how food boutiques work: they go to the same grocery as you, and buy the same groceries as you. Here's the difference: *they unwrap it.* That's really about it. The boutiquiers unwrap the food, sell you a fourth as much, and charge you eight times as much.

And we wonder why we're never visited by intelligent life from other planets.

Adults, of course, just look at me with that "bless his heart" look - the one that expresses their frank amazement that I've made it to my age, alive and unmaimed. ("Barry, don't butter the bagel toward you neck, dear.") Adults will tilt their heads, like Snow White picking up a particularly clumsy Dwarf, and remind me: "well, you can always freeze it!"

But freezing leads to thawing, and thawing wants doing well in advance of eating, and that involves that 'p' thing...I forget what it's called. Oh, yeah, I remember. Planning.

So, rather than clutter the garbage or clog the disposal, I feed the fauna. Living beyond my backyard tree line are many animals: deer, at least one fox family, a few feral cats that whine, strut, and mewl, endlessly. (Either they have Hollywood affiliations, or the animal kingdom has a Congress.)

Rarely does a day go by when I'm not out on the deck, carrying something currently or formerly edible to catapult toward the tree line. On any given day, the launch menu could be two-day-old pizza, three-week-old cheese, or six-month-old Wheat Thins. Or I may find some forgotten something *behind* something else in my pantry, something that's been there so long it's actually mad at me, something with an expiration date so old it was written in Roman numerals.

To be sure, running my own little forest catering business makes *me* feel good, but I'm not sure I'm doing the animals any favors, at least not from a Food Nazi perspective. The fox, in particular, is starting to look a little jowly. I mean, I've been lobbing them leftovers for so long, the animals have formed a little woodlands weight management support group. In fact, the last time the vixen waddled out of the tree line to score a discarded 'everything' bagel, I'm pretty sure I saw her holding a tub of Ranch dip and a TV remote control.

So, if you're out there, and you're interested in a non-committal commitment, and you didn't eat yet, give me a call.

But let it ring - I may be in the gym, spotting for the vixen.

Everybody Loves a Fee Circus

The American mortgage. Welcome to the machine.
<>~<>~~~~~~~~~~<>~<>~~~~~~~~~~<>~<>

I just bought my house again.

Technically, the term for the self-inflicted wounding I just went through is a "refinance," according to the governing authority that controls these things, the AARG (American Association of Realty Gougers).

Here in America, (re)financing a home has traditionally been a fairly common business transaction, one that takes place thousands of times every year. It's a simple thing: buyer (*A*) wants to buy house (*B*) from owner (*C*) using money borrowed from lender (*D*), but only after *A* pays 743 million dollars (*$*) in obscure but mandatory fees (*$*@&#!*) to legions of evil leeches (*AARG*).

But lately, thanks to a psychotic Congress who decided that a unemployment check should qualify as "proof of income" (yes, that did actually happen), buying a house has gone from being ridiculously simple to ... well, to simply ridiculous.

As a public school student might say, "like, the pendulum done swung and stuff."

So let's break it all down.

The Back Story

Normally, in my world, a financial transaction is not something that excites. Due to the fact that I don't understand money, my interest in money-related activities is limited to simple, functional conversations:

- How much is that TV?
- No, seriously.
- You're insane.

Nevertheless, even someone as investment-ignorant as I can grasp that a home loan at 3% is better than one at 6. I think. But, for the last 6-7 years, I've consistently, unfailingly made the mistake of paying my mortgage on time, so I don't qualify for the government's badger-like interloping ... I mean, um, beneficent intervention.

But finally, somebody somewhere screwed up and allowed a humane lender to stay in business. We met; we got along; we ran some quick preliminary numbers; nobody brought up any uncomfortable concepts, like "excess collateral," or "Faust." Things looked promising. Finally!

And the dance continued.

The Appraisal

If it weren't for the jaw-dropping "bill for services rendered" I received later, this part of the dance might have skipped my attention entirely. From a space-time-continuum perspective, the appraisal wasn't really an event. It was more like a sighting.

An appraisal is the process by which all the Home Purchase players come to an agreement on the value of the house ($3), except for the assessors at the local taxing authority, who use their own arcane calculations ($249,500,000).

The purpose of the appraisal is simple: to ensure that you do not qualify for a refinance. (This is part of the dance.) But what you *will* qualify for is a *conditional* refinance. In other words, somebody *will* agree to lend you the money you need, but only if you borrow *more* money than you need. The "more" part is something known as PMI, an acronym that stands for "Pirate Money Incentives."

To understand how PMI works, imagine that you're dangling from a plane by your seatbelt. A flight attendant offers to pull you back into the plane, for fifty bucks. (She also offers you a snack - a bag containing four peanuts.) You agree to the fifty, and thank her for the peanuts. But then she bumps her fee to sixty.

What're you gonna do? As a single guy, dangling from a plane with three peanuts, you have two possible responses:

1. Okay! Sixty it is!
2. Aaaiiiiieeeehhhhhhh!!!

The person who actually puts together the appraisal is a completely unbiased, fully independent professional, except on Earth, where his credentials are a bit more succinct. ("This is my brother-in-law's boy, Louie.") As best as I can tell, it's only a formality for the appraiser to actually show up at your property. The "appraising" part, they could do from their computer at home. Effectively, the appraisal is based on some complex ratio, involving something called "comps." (literal translation: *"number of active meth labs in your neighborhood"*)

And based on his bill, and the time the lad physically spent on my property, if this kid works a solid 40-hour week, young Louie's pulling down about 450 large - *a month.*

In my case, the appraiser showed up, took a few photos, walked once around the house, made a phone call to confirm his appointment at a yacht dealership, and then left.

Mmm hmm. Don't tell *me* the economy's in trouble.

The Underwriters

If I barely saw the appraiser as he whisked by, I never saw the underwriters at all. All these faceless ghouls ever did, day after day, was demand documents. More documents. Older documents. Additional documents.

I think they were eating them. I think the Underwriters were metabolizing my documents.

Since I haven't used a fax machine since, oh, the Reformation, I spent hours scanning pages, saving them as PDFs, and emailing them. (to the lender, not directly to the Underwriters - I don't think the Under-kind hold up well in daylight, if you catch my drift...)

I mean, these document-digesting creatures were insatiable. At one point, I actually had this phone conversation with the underwriters:

Me: Hello?

(Faint sound of firewood crackling, and chants)

UW: We have received your IRS calculation worksheets packet, fiscal year 1961, for non-loadbearing Iberian farm pond algae allowances and curd disposal fees.

Me: I thought you might. You know, since I sent it and all.

UW: We're missing page 3 of 8.

Me: I didn't send that page. That page contains nothing but the words "This page intentionally left blank."

UW: We want page 3.

Me: Seriously. You want me to scan and send you a blank page.

UW: We want page 3. We want page 3. We want page 3.

(Faint thrumming sound of a tanned-hide drum)

The Paperwork

This is the bloody part. This is the part where you, the lendee, discover that there's a world muttering beneath your world, a sleepless realm populated by pitiless parasites: the Fee Banshees.

Over the years, thousands of these relentless nickel-and-dimer demons have wormed their way into the mortgage process, and they all want a bite. There are fees to file documents, fees to re-file documents, fees to notarize documents, fees to prove that fees were paid to notarize documents. It's as if events were bound up in a new Newton's Law: for every transaction, there is a an unequal and obstinate transaction.

Clerk fees, court fees, half-court fees. Print fees, fax fees, stamp fees. And my personal favorite: the flood plain fee. That's right - I have to pay a fee ... *again* ... to prove that, in the last 6-7 years, my house has not been relocated to the banks of the Dead Sea, or New Orleans' Ninth Ward.

And it's non-negotiable ... you *have* to pay the fee. It doesn't matter if your property hasn't seen two consecutive days of rainfall since Noah paired up the platypi. You have to pay the fee.

Ultimately, however, the Underwriter Undead will wrap up the paperwork and provide you with the grail: something known as the "Good Faith Estimate."

Good Faith Estimate. There are many problems with this term. Let's iterate:

- Good: no, it isn't

44

- Faith: no, you haven't
- Estimate: (literal translation: *"whatever the original number was, add three zeroes to it"*)

Of course, you know as well as I know that these reams of forms will never be seen again in the history of history. Ever. They're doomed to dissolve in some dark, cavernous Siberia-sized "Raiders of the Lost Ark" government warehouse, a facility funded by some opaque Pentagon budget line item, like the "National Helium Emergency Reserves," or the "NATO Pan-National Effort to Fund Joe Biden's Supply of Teeth Whitener."

Unless the documents are discovered by the Underwriter Undead.

The Closing

The closing itself was a dream. We began on time and wrapped up quickly. The lawyers had pre-scoured the planet, gathering up every remaining sheet of paper on Earth uneaten by the Underwriter Undead, and I scribbled my signature on every single one of them. During that thirty minutes, I gave out more autographs than Jane Fonda at an NVA reunion.

In fact, during the entire closing, there was only one snag: for some reason, the lawyers insisted I sign my name in blue ink, rather than using my ever-present black ink-filled Uni-Ball. Odd, but - okay. Suddenly, the conference room door blew open, and in popped the Rarely Reverend Al Sharpton, yelling something about ink racism, quill quotas, and an irrefutable blue pen bias. Fortunately, a quick-thinking lawyer lobbed a microphone out a nearby window, and you know how Al gets when he sees a microphone. The Rarely Reverend cleared the window, leapt to the lawn, and we wrapped things up.

I said 'thanks' to the refinancers, hopped in my car, and drove to my new old home, where me and my trusty Uni-Ball will live in peace. At least, for a few years, until we're advised - again - to refinance. Until then - adieu.

Or, as a public school graduate might say, "until we, like, meet again, and stuff."

Skullburn

More fun ways to frighten timid people

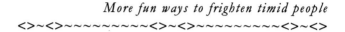

Earlier this year, while I wasn't looking, I got blindsided by another birthday. They're relentless, these birthday things - I could swear I just had one last year.

Generally speaking, I'm a big fan of birthdays, especially the 'milestone' years. If you're a guy, the milestone years are very cool. You know the list:

- Year One: You've made it! You're breathing, your parents have submitted your resume and references to several exclusive kindergartens, and you're safe from any retroactive Roe v. Wade issues, unless you vote Republican.
- Year Eighteen: You're not old enough to have a beer, but you're old enough to go point guns at brown people in some sandbox with a name like Absurdistan.
- Year Thirty: You're in a mortgage, but you're out of testosterone.

But once you get past thirty or forty years of this, you find yourself celebrating more, well, *obscure* annual victories:

- You've made it to the next prime number
- You've made it another year without clipping cents-off 'Depends' coupons

Personally, I've tried to benchmark the last few, um, prime numbers a bit differently. As each birthday rolls around, I try to deliver on a couple of personal goals:

- Do something I've never done before
- Avoid seeing my name in the obituary column

Here's the problem: the list of things I've never done before is shrinking. The legal list, anyway. And at my age, illegal things no longer hold any allure. Other than one marginally actionable incident involving a staggeringly gorgeous bartender from Illinois and a bitter ferret from Charleston, I've studiously avoided activities that might result in me having to say things like "Yes, Your Honor" and end up wearing loose-fitting state-issue clothing.

So this year, I shaved my head.

Ever done that? It was a lot more difficult than I expected. I mean, we're talking about my brain's veneer versus my cheesy twelve-pack of chin scrapers. I consider myself very lucky to have gotten out alive, with only two new divots in my head.

You Gonna Finish That Dragon?

It wasn't just that there was more real estate to survey, more lawn to mow. It was like invading a foreign country, with no maps and minimal ordnance. I mean, think about it: you're attacking your own skull with a razor you bought at the grocers for 79 cents. Plus, this isn't at all like shaving your face, or your chin, or a coastal ferret, something you've done maybe 10,000 times before (not the ferret).

This was a trip to rural head. This was crania incognita.

And because I'm approximately as coordinated as a damaged mollusk, I can only use one hand to do *anything*, which usually doesn't slow me down very much, unless I need to clap. But when I was trying to shave my head, even my 'good' hand seemed to have a mind of its own. I spent long minutes staring at my reflection in the bathroom mirror, trying to communicate non-lethal razoring vectors to my wrist, so that I wouldn't gash my brain wagon and suddenly become what is known as 'breaking news.'

But since you're reading this, you probably figured out that I survived the deforestation. It took forever, but I survived. After the scrape-tivities, I dried my dome and dabbed at the divots. I threw out the razor and threw on a hospital scrub shirt. And lastly, I took a few moments for review and introspection.

My first surprise in the mirror, once the mission had been completed, was that I looked like an escaped mental patient from some particularly sadistic future. There's just something about a freshly-shaved, pale-blue-tinted top-skull that screams *"Nurse Ratched! I want my cigarettes!"*

Looking back, maybe the scrub shirt was a bad idea.

And my de-pelted skull wasn't at all what I'd expected. I'd always assumed that, under the hair, I'd been carting around a coy but structurally perfect geodesic masterpiece, sure to bring an envious tear to the eye of Buckminster Fuller and any other bowling ball manufacturers.

But no. My unveiled over-veined head bulges in the back, like that short-tempered she-beast from the *Alien* movies; you know, that bucket-headed drool-monster with the 'live and let live' personality of the Queen of Hearts, the territorial management style of Leona Helmsley, and the deluxe dental plan of Joe Biden.

So be warned, all you potential head denuders. Your bush-hogged bean is *not* perfect. But that only makes sense, considering the body your head is sitting on.

It gets worse. Wait till that first time you expose your Carlsbad Cavernized pale pate to the sun at the beach. You can practically hear old Sol snickering, "Oh, the things I'm gonna do to that head!" And then, après skullburn, good luck trying to find a nice, unscented, anti-glare, SPF 8000 ointment.

On the other hand...

The Upside of Cranial Strip-Mining

- If you're single and still spouse shopping, being hairless attracts a whole new dating niche: the free-lance phrenologist.

- You can rent out the additional skull space for billboard signage. Keep it tasteful -- polite society tends to frown on three-dimensional cows with bad spelling skills hawing heterosexual chicken biscuits.
- If a passing bird decides to, well, jettison anything, at least it won't land in your hair.

It'd be okay if you could harvest your head and then spend a few prime numbered solar cycles coming to terms with your new neck marble. But eventually you have to leave the house, because although as a country we've figured out how to land on the moon, we still can't get anybody to deliver Mexican food.

And you newly nude-capped guys should know this: bald evokes commentary. When faced with the suddenly shorn, the general public refuses to go quietly into that bald night. Co-workers will bombard you with their sudden repertoire of 'baldy' jokes, that they consider hilarious to the point of Pulitzer nomination.

No worries. Should the jokes get out of hand, just send in the ferret.

Theoretically, though, there is social potential in being close-cropped. I'm told that many women consider a bald head to be virile. That's certainly true in my case, assuming 'virile' means 'appears to have lost a fight with a multi-bladed farm implement.'

But, like most things, it'll all work out. If things get desperate, I can always phone the coast, call in a favor, and staple on a ferret toupee.

After all, it seems to work for Joe Biden.

Ward Cleaver's Coyote Weekend

Remember, kids...and men with kids...don't try this at home!

<>~<>~~~~~~~~~<>~<>~~~~~~~~~~~<>~<>

Last weekend, I saved a man's life. Which gives you some idea of just how far I'm willing to go, on any given weekend, to avoid mowing the lawn.

Now, to you, saving somebody's life may not be a big deal. Maybe you run around saving people's lives all the time. For all I know, you regularly inject yourself in other people's business, like one of those meddling masked superheroes, or some buttinski functionary from the Federal Bureau of Kibitzers and Samaritans. Or you could be lying to us. Maybe you've never saved a life your whole life. I have no way of knowing, 'cause I don't know you. For Pete's sake, I just made you up less than 30 seconds ago.

But for me, saving a fellow human being's life -- and doing it *on a weekend* -- well, that's a major accomplishment for a guy who won't buy an entire carton of eggs for fear of making a commitment ... for someone whose idea of 'strenuous exercise' is driving to get Chinese food instead of having it delivered.

Here's how it happened. A married friend of mine posted on facebook that he was 'playing bachelor' for the weekend. His wife was leaving town to attend some social event that involved mature, civilized adults, so, wisely, she went alone. But by leaving her husband at home alone, she'd created a volatile situation. Bad juju. An element in an unstable state. Def-Con Four. A twenty-third-hour Jack Bauer moment.

Imagine it - a married man, suddenly on his own. A husband with no instructions. No 'how to' coping manual, no navigational primer for day-to-day life. A male spouse, sans commands. Imagine a fish out of water. Imagine an antelope, having spent its entire life in a zoo, being released into the wild. Imagine Bill Clinton in Cartagena. Imagine an Indonesian dog in the presence of a peckish young Barack Obama.

Right away, I knew my friend was veering to trouble because of that comment he'd casually tossed - the one about 'playing bachelor.' What a rookie remark! He thought that being single, even for a few days, was a transition someone could just slip into without consequence, like not shaving, or listening to Zamfir, master of the pan flute.

No! It takes years (and bloody years they can be) before bachelors learn how to survive without parents, spouses, or ironed shirts. So I knew that it was just a matter of time before my friend crashed and sank, and I would need to sling him a buoy.

Quickly, inevitably, he hit the wall. And there on facebook, he posted a proper, honest yelp for help:

You Gonna Finish That Dragon?

"What do bachelors eat?"

So, I tossed the buoy. And saved a life. Of course, I had a little fun along the way...

~~.~~.~~.~~

Q: My wife's out of town, and it's lunchtime, and I don't see any food. I've heard her mention some room called a 'pantry,' but I don't know where it is. Besides, it could be locked, and even if I *did* know where it was, there can't be any cooked food in there, 'cause I'd be able to smell it. See? I'm smart like that. Mind like a steel trap. I got this whole 'bachelor' thing bagged and tagged. But what am I supposed to eat?

A: Check your freezer, call somebody that delivers, or head for a drive-thru. (There's probably a grocery nearby, but I don't recommend such desperate measures on your first solo flight.) Generally, food comes from colorful boxes in your freezer. Just microwave the box until its contents achieve the texture of a monitor lizard, the temperature of moving lava, and the color of George Hamilton. If you'd rather, you can get pizza delivered by gaunt young people with face piercings, or get Chinese food delivered by people who, for some reason, are never Chinese. Alternatively, you can get food (of a sort) from the sliding-glass window cut in the side of a drive-thru, handed directly to you through your car window. This common, window-to-window transfer is how we get what is known as 'fast food,' which may be the most egregious oxymoron ever, because 'fast food' is neither. But at least you won't starve.

~~-~~-~~-~~

Q: But there aren't any plates or forks on the table. Where do I eat?

A: Over the sink, of course, like any career single guy. Or, if you're feeling sparky, go wild. Be a coyote. Devolve! Abandon your status as a civilized, trousered ape and ... ready? ... *eat on the sofa! Without a napkin!* Cower in unshaven rooms in underwear, and burn your money in wastebaskets! Howl! *Howl!*

(Thanks, Allen Ginsberg)

~~-~~-~~-~~

Q: I'm all out of clean shirts. I'm out of kinda-clean shirts, too, 'cause the one I've been wearing all week moved out. Apparently it achieved consciousness, walked away, and has been spotted at the State Park, attacking random campers wearing permanent-press Tommy Bahamas. How do I make clean clothes? Does it involve that pantry thing?

A: You know that little room, off the kitchen, with the door that leads to the garage? That tiny, closet-y room with the coat rack and the brooms? Yes, brooms. *BROOMS.* B-R-O. . . never mind. Ever noticed those two boxy white machines against the wall in that room? Yes, the machi ... forget I asked. Look, here's what some guys do: just donate the dirty shirt to Goodwill. Overnight, they'll clean it and toss it on a hanger. Next day, go back to Goodwill and buy your shirt back for two bucks. Everybody wins: Goodwill gets a $2 sale, you get a tax deduction *and* a clean shirt, and you saved several bucks on dry cleaning. Dry cleaning. *DRY CLEANING.* D-R- .. never mind.

~~-~~-~~-~~

So. The next time you see a more-or-less clean-shaven fellow at the grocery, a man wearing a glazed shirt and an equally glazed expression who's nursing a bag of russets and a jar of bacon bits, a man who's numbly staring at the 250 brands of bottled Ranch salad dressing, have a little mercy. Show a little compassion.

Because there before you stands a Temporary Bachelor. A married guy, whose wife is out of town. A clueless, cue-less sojourner, who's learning how to be a coyote.

And he's about to eat an undercooked baked potato.

Barry Parham

Hey, We're Two, Too!

"I now pronounce you man and wife and wife and wife."
<>~<>~~~~~~~~~~<>~<>~~~~~~~~~~~<>~<>

It's not fair. It's just not right. There I was, sitting at home and minding my own single guy business, when suddenly some whining psychotic starts yelling at me online.

Look. If I wanted whining psychotics to yell at me, I'd start dating again.

But there he was - some faceless guy sending me Twitter messages, demanding (see *'whining'*) I support him in his quest to marry multiple people. (see *'psychotic'*)

Ooh. Where do I sign.

Now, I know what you're probably thinking. You're probably thinking this online petitioner was just one more marginally-stable male with a manifesto; just the latest self-diagnosed tragic hero; just another 21-to-34-year-old guy speared with a few ounces of oddly-situated face jewelry, who drinks bulk-priced beer and smells like bulk-priced cheese, is dressed in a checkered hunting shirt, gym shorts, & athletic socks, and lives

59

in his parent's dimly lit basement with a refurbished Apple laptop and a forgery-accessed Ritalin prescription.

But no. This guy (I'll call him Lipids) had also put together a nice basket of logical (see *'raging sarcasm'*) arguments in favor of his effort, a cause that he's christened 'Plural Marriage.'

(Lipids is what, in the sixties, we would've called an *'activist'* or, as we know it today, a *'schmuck.'*)

See, Lipids thinks it's downright discriminatory that several consenting adults aren't allowed to marry each other, all at the same time, even optimistically assuming that they're all sane. (see *'Pollyanna Syndrome'*)

So Lipids and his lieutenants are fighting for group marriage equality rights (see *'tax breaks'*), while ignoring the societal implications of such massive relationship-based redistricting. I mean, just for a start, allowing a whole gang of people to marry each other would call for a complete rethinking of that whole 'bridal registry' thing.

Or, on a less mercenary level, imagine this: one husband, living in a house with seven or eight wives, all sharing (or not) one bathroom. Poor guy would have to grow another bladder.

And speaking of the ol' Fortress of Solitude, how about all those monogrammed hand towels? Hmm? Since the dawn of time ... or at least the dawn of Target ... those little towels have been sold in just-so sets, His and Hers. Haven't thought about *that* little detail, have you? *Hmm?* I didn't think so.

Nonetheless, Lipids and the Spousettes are demanding his/her/their equal access to entitlement money, which is what people do these days instead of working. See, according to these Pluralistas, marriage is a fundamental human right, right up there with a free cell phone, or being allowed to unload your idling car in the airport's "Taxis Only" lane.

Hey, it's in the Constitution. Look it up.

From there, Lipids segued into a debating point that even I thought was obscure, and I make up stuff for a living. Plural Guy's next postulate was based on the following iffy, oddly-spelled premise: "Humans are not animals on Noah's Arc. Two by two is nonsense."

Ooh. Touché.

It is a point that may or may not sway potential Pluralites, but it does confirm a few things:

- Lipids has never been mistaken for a returning Jeopardy champion.
- Apparently, Noah and menagerie survived the flood by hunkering down in part of a circle's circumference.
- Lipids missed his 3pm dose of Ritalin.

But the overarching argument of the macro-managing Many-Mates is this: the more love in the home, the more stability in society.

Sorry, Lipids.

Nice idea, but you're assuming that more people shoved in the same place would somehow automagically equal more harmony, even though one of them hasn't seen the inside of a bathroom in twelve years. That's like saying the more people in the car, the better the freeway traffic.

And Team Lipids isn't settling for simple polygyny, either. This is not just some chauvinistic "me and my harem" movement. In the Plural Marriage handbook, anything goes: a man and two or three women; two men or two women; two men *and* two women; three women and two men; one woman and seven dwarfs; five men and Grace Jones - the possibilities are rich.

By the way: in this type of discussion, it's usually around this point that people start fretting about something they call the "slippery slope." (Usually these people are conservatives. Conservatives, as a rule, want to avoid heading down a "slippery slope." Liberals, on the other hand, are always averse to opening a "can of worms.")

But these multi-betrothal big-tent mathematics come in handy for simpatico recruiting purposes, too. According to one Plural Marriage supporter - a strange spotted-faced female named Dave - two out of three people in a plural marriage will be the same sex! So the Neo-Nuptialites are mano a mano with the LGBT community, too! (Of course, the 2-outta-3 rule does not take San Francisco into account. At last count, Frisco had more recognized genders than Joe Biden has original teeth.)

LGBT, of course, collectively refers to the Lesbian, Gay, Bisexual, and Transgender community. It used to go by the acronym LGB (less than/greater than/both), not to be confused with RGB (genders that have been Photoshopped) or the KGB (Russian grooms posing as Russian brides). The term LGBT was originally coined by an off-campus clothing chain known as The Gap. Roughly translated from the original San Fernando Valley-speak, LGBT means "If it moves, date it." *(Source: the lost scrolls of, like, Santa Monica and stuff)*

The LGBT are a subgroup of AOI (Alternately-Oriented Individuals) who may or may not suffer from GID (Gender Identity Disorder), a condition recognized by the APA (American Psychiatric Association) as part of the AAA. (Absurd Array of Acronyms)

Ultimately, of course, given that I'm a single guy with no social acronyms whatsoever, I opted out of Lipids' offer of solidarity. But I do wish him all the best, as he continues on his mission to collect enough in-laws to field his own NCAA football team. And from everything I've heard about in-laws, he's gonna need all the padding he can get.

Not to mention some more Ritalin.

Barry Parham

Norman Gets Written Up

Excellence is okay, in moderation

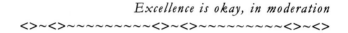

After an eight-year absence, I've recently injected myself back into corporate America. This was largely due to circumstances beyond my control, like the economy, and wanting to eat.

There was also the small matter of maddening micro-management by an out-of-control federal bureaucracy, a government that apparently won't be satisfied until they're regulating which direction you face when trimming your nails. (followed by filing IRS Form 10.7-B 3c to cover your quarterly Emery Board Use Tax for Non-Farm Use)

See, for nearly eight years, I've been working from home, which is great, except for the...uh...except for the...mmm...well, never mind. There *is* no "except." Working from home is great. Period. Heck, just being able to use your own *bathroom* is worth a buck.

So, after so many years of no commutes, minimal interruptions, and occasionally not wearing pants, it was a bit of a gloomy trudge back to the rat sprint; rodent race; ferret relay; whatever they call it - I forget already. I was not at all looking forward to foregoing freedoms like going out to the beach on a moment's whim, or, as I like to call it, "working remotely."

And now, an entire year has passed, and I've had my first "employee annual review," administered by this weird guy from HR who is perversely protective of his stapler. (It's a Swingline, red model. It's actually quite nice.)

For those of you who are too rich to work, or accountable to no one, or are otherwise associated with the US Congress, an "employee annual review" is one of those HR Department-mandated exercises, like Ugly Sweater Day, or signing a release form in which you agree to pretend that you actually *read* the Employee Handbook, a document which experts will agree is the dullest read in the history of mankind, with the exception of an Al Gore speech. Here's how it works:

Your supervisor / team lead / boss spends several hours staring at several bulleted lists packed with psychotherapeutic mumble-speak, like this:

- Encourages cross-functional collaboration
- Participates in postulating positively-reinforced paradigms
- Bathes

After your boss regains consciousness, s/he just googles "top ten employee review," copies a few canned responses into your review, and signs her/his name. Then the boss repeats the process for everybody else in the department. And that's why you often see eleven different co-workers all described as "competent with existing methodologies, effusively self-motivated, and largely lice-free."

Under the corporate covers, annual reviews are all about good employees. Bad employees, of course, are sacrosanct. You're just stuck with the bad ones, 'cause they'll sue you. And every company has their share - people like Linda, the Noxious Perfume Cloud Monster, or Chad from Sales, who's forever blocking the bloody hallways because he's having conversations with real people while he takes imaginary golf swings, over and over, until you want to stab him in his tanned throat.

Employee Review season is an interesting thing to watch - a dog's breakfast of diplomacy, chess, and restraint. The trick is to make good employees look good - *but not too good*. Too good is not good for anyone involved. In corporate America, at least on the sub-executive levels, it's better to become wonderful slowly.

So let's take a quick look at some of the secret code used in the Employee Review process - let's decipher some differences between what they say...and what they really mean.

~-~-~-~-~-~

When they say "Is adaptable and flexible"
What they mean: Collin shows up for work on most days, and is almost never missing any relevant pieces of clothing.

When they say "Demonstrates sound business ethics"

What they mean: I have never caught Norman carrying boxes of office equipment out to his car.

When they say "Handles confidential information appropriately"
What they mean: In Marketing meetings, Tamblyn is always discreet when pointing out to Chad from Sales that he missed a little white spot there under his nose.

When they say "Places a high value on 'It's the right thing to do'"
What they mean: When demoing software to multi-billion-dollar accounts, Mandy carefully avoids phrases like "glaring logical error that's gonna cost thousands and delay release by several months," opting for the more succinct "minor glitch."

When they say "Treats co-workers with respect"
What they mean: Needs work. Once, when stuck in the elevator with Linda and her yak-gagging Perfume Cloud, Todd allegedly commented, "Whoa! Is that *you*, or is somebody stewing pickles?"

When they say "Maintains a healthy balance between work and personal interests"
What they mean: Norman is an active member of the community. He teaches a class in full-contact macramé, he volunteers at the juvenile female prison, and he has one of the finest collections of red staplers I've ever seen.

When they say "Acts consistently with company values and principles"
What they mean: I have not personally witnessed Walter abusing any farm animals, during business hours.

When they say "Possesses up-to-date technical/functional knowledge"

You Gonna Finish That Dragon?

What they mean: It's not unusual to see Chad from Sales texting during meetings, or while driving, or while showering, or while undergoing open chest cavity surgery. Chad from Sales is a seriously obsessed gadget freak. I mean, to the point of needing an intervention. Some kind of analog rehab. This guy stares at his smart phone so intently that I wonder if his soul is trapped in there.

When they say "Holds self personally accountable"
What they mean: Needs work. Well, on the last two words, anyway.

When they say "Listens to others"
What they mean: *Pardon? What? HA HA HA HA HA HA HA HA HA HA.*
HR: *Get over yourself.*
Annual Review: *I'm sorry.*

When they say "Pursues challenging goals"
What they mean: Sally still thinks that her shameless flirting with Chad from Sales will pay off, despite her having an overbite that would make George Romero drool.

When they say "Accurately assesses resource needs"
What they mean: Martina realizes, like everybody else in this hope-forsaken "department that time forgot," that the chances of us ever actually *getting* those new monitors we were promised are about as good as the chances I'll grow an extra larynx.

When they say "Makes decisions under uncertain conditions"

What they mean: Needs work. Tiraldo once spent forty-five anxious minutes staring at the vending machine, muttering "Baby Ruth. Snickers. Baby Ruth. Snickers. Baby R..."

When they say "Brings perspectives and approaches together"
What they mean: *Huh? Bring which and what where? We have no idea what this means - and neither do YOU. Stop it.*
HR: *Keep it up, smart mouth! Keep it up! Have you SEEN the stack of resumes on my desk? We'll drop you faster than Joe Biden at a 'Jeopardy' audition.*
Annual Review: *I'm sorry. Really.*
HR: *Hey! Is that my stapler?*

When they say "Respects fellow workers and shared work environments"
What they mean: Roz, I'm told, appears to have prescriptions for all those tablets, which she's careful to keep wrapped in tin foil, safely away from her co-workers. Especially Chad in Sales.

~-~-~-~-~-~

At any rate, I think I survived my first annual review. We'll see. I'd hate to have to give up eating.

But if things don't work out, maybe I can barter with the grocery. What's the current street value of a red Swingline stapler?

You Gonna Finish That Dragon?

Raw fish. Well, after the hot wine, we probably should've seen that coming.

<>~<>~~~~~~~~~~<>~<>~~~~~~~~~~~<>~<>

Here's something you almost never hear: "Could I have some more eel?"

This past week, for the first time ever, I intentionally ordered sushi. (Yes, intentionally. Once, I ordered some raw tuna by mistake, but I was in some dimly-lit sadisti-cafe where the shameless proprietors called raw fish 'tapas.' Fortunately, the foul place was pipe-bombed by a vagrant group of Metrogendered Vampire Bikers on Projectile Dancing Night.)

Now, I've lived a lot of years, and done a lot of things, many of them legal. But until this past week, I'd never tried sushi. Nothing personal, you understand. It's mostly been a matter of Single Guy Ignorance, combined with a localized unavailability. See, here in upstate South Carolina, if the grocery advertises a special on sushi, that usually means the motor in their 'Refrigerated' section died again.

But last week, some friends invited me along for an evening at their favorite sushi eatery, and I wanted to go - I just didn't know how to behave once I got there. All I knew from sushi was what I'd overheard: it involved rice and raw fish.

I had no problem with the 'rice' part. At rice, I sneer. I face rice like a man.

Crossword puzzles had taught me to expect eel and seaweed, too, which I unashamedly declare are two food groups I can do without, raw or otherwise.

So I'd been kind of a sushi agnostic ... no real attraction or animus - I just hoped it didn't exist. And I was clueless - I didn't know the menu, the portions, the procedures, the prices. I didn't know why people employed the phrase 'sushi grade tuna' instead of the perfectly functional word 'raw.' I didn't know if they'd have forks, or if I'd be forced to figure out how to poke food at my face using a pair of those wooden knitting needles that severe women shove in their hair buns. I didn't know how to say "Heimlich Maneuver" in Japanese.

Plus, I'd always heard that eating undercooked stuff could cause you to experience health insurance issues, like pre-existing conditions, or death. And I've just never been a huge fan of anything, food or not, where the primary goal is to not die.

But I still wanted to join my friends (and not die). So I decided to rehearse. I was travelling on business at the time, so I found one of the city's sushi bars on the internet, spent a while studying the restaurant's posted photos, looking for anyone doing the Heimlich, and then dropped in for a test lunch.

The restaurant I found online was named Tsunami, which I thought was an interesting marketing decision. I mean, you can search the Michelin Red Guide for quite some time without finding a five-star restaurant named after a natural disaster.

But, as I pointed out before, I fear no restaurant's rice. I wade through rice like a Titan. So I lashed down my car, boarded up the windows, battened down the hatchback, and went in.

Thinking back, the restaurant's online ad seemed to have been grasping a bit. Beyond the sushi-specific menu, they weren't left with many bragging points:

- Non-sushi menu
- Waiter service
- Parking lot

What they *don't* tell you about their heralded 'waiter service' is that the person doing all the waiting is *you*. Good grief, what a wait! It was like dining at a chophouse staffed by the Department of Motor Vehicles. By the time they brought my lunch, I'd forgotten what city I was in. The food took so long, General Tso had retired with pension.

I still don't know what the problem was; I mean, how long can it take to not cook fish?

Sushi, according to the internet, is an ancient Japanese word, complex in meaning, but roughly translated as "more stuff we can sell Americans for an 8,000-percent markup." Sushi was actually developed sometime in the Eighth Century in Southeast Asia, before it got bought by Sony and imported to Japan.

The original concoction consisted of freshly-captured fish, salted and then wrapped in lacto-fermented rice, and may I say for the record that if you know a nastier food-related term than 'lacto-fermented,' please keep it to yourself.

Meanwhile, back at the practice restaurant: the food was very good, but the menu alone was worth the visit. It had obviously been written by someone for whom English was a second language, like Gollum, or Joe Biden. The word 'special' had been misspelled, and they'd managed to spell the word 'sesame' three different ways, which is hard to do on one sheet of paper.

I believe there should be some kind of qualifying test. I don't think a person should be allowed to open a restaurant if they can't spell the word 'special.' That's like appointing somebody to run the Treasury Department who can't fill out his own taxes. Okay, bad example.

From my brief experience with it, sushi is prepared as follows:

- Flatten a seaweed leaf, or however you say 'seaweed leaf' in damp botany
- Grab the nearest at-hand green vegetable and long-cut it into 3-4 tiny pole vault poles
- Dice up a filet of fish so freshly dead that it could still vote in Chicago

- Collect the tiny track-and-field veggies and the almost-probably-not-toxic fish parts and roll it all up in the seaweed frondifolia green cigar thingy
- Knit a snug little rice sweater around it
- Cut the concoction into small hockey puck portions, so they look like bone cross-sections that somebody nicked from med school on Spinal Cord Day
- Serve with forty-two sauces whose names all end in the letter 'I'
- Charge $80

Other than the Daily Speicals (sic), the expansive menu also spoke of a tofu salad, made from 'very healthy tofu.' (Somewhere near the restaurant, I take it, there's a high-impact bean curd gym.) And many of the menu items come with some side called miso soup, or you can opt for a house salad with 'steam or fried rice.'

Now, I like a good salad, but I hate it when the 'waiter service' just globs dollops of steam all over the thing. I always ask if I can get the steam on the side.

One can also order, though not pronounce, a dish called Yaki Udon, which was described as 'pan stir fried noodles with vegi.' Interestingly, you can also order Vegetable Yaki Udon - kind of like asking for a salad salad with a side of salad. ("Hold the steam, please - I'm on a diet.")

Another entrée, edamame, sounds tempting, but when you peel back the mask, it's actually a plate of lightly salted boiled soybeans, which is why they call it edamame.

The menu referenced something called a Volcano Roll, which is the kind of stunt you could only pull off in a restaurant named after a tidal wave. But the menu made no mention of Godzilla, Mothra, or Rodan, though I did notice dragon. (At that point, of course, I signaled for my 'waiter service' and asked, "Is that free-range dragon? Or corn-fed?" No reply. Nothing. Death. The 'waiter service' must have left her sense of humor in the 'Parking lot.')

And leave room for dessert! For afters, you can finish up with some nice green tea ice cream. Mmm.

But I learned important lessons:

- You can eat sushi and not die.
- You can eat in a sushi restaurant and not have to eat sushi at all.
- Everything on a sushi menu is not necessarily sushi, you backwoods troll, you.

In fact, as I learned from the internet, sushi really only refers to the rice. The actual rolls (the tubes inside those tight-fitting rice cardigans) are called *yukiwa-maki*. What sushi fans call 'hand rolls' are known as *temaki sushi*, fish served without the rice insulation is called *sashimi*, and fish that can surf the internet and wear cardigans on the beach are referred to as *Franki Avaloni*.

And in a related story - my lunch-time crossword puzzle this week led me to some interesting facts about other Pacific-

You Gonna Finish That Dragon?

Polynesian cultures, including Hawaii, our 57th State and one of the three birthplaces of President Barack Hussein Obama I.

As you probably know, the Hawaiian language is a Polynesian dialect, comprised of a collection of power vowels, with the occasional consonant thrown in to let you know a new word has started. With the exception of the odd 'h' or 'm', Hawaiian seems to consist largely of just the vowels *a, e, i, o,* and *u*. In fact, *'aeiou'* (pronounced 'ow') is actually a word in Hawaii - it means "remind me next time to let that pork cool a while first."

The word *Polynesian* (literally, *'many nesians'*) is an ancient pre-tourism term, said to have been coined by the first foreigner to visit Hawaii, Captain Kangaroo, an unimaginably white man who also gave us the terms *Indonesia* ('dog sushi'), *Micronesia* ('Johnny Depp'), and *amnesia* ('Richard Nixon'). The bold Captain wrapped up his wildly successful Hawaiian tour by getting eaten, after which historians Anglicized his name to Cook.

Like our other Polynesian friends, Hawaiians eat a lot of sea-harvested food, too, but they're not in as big a hurry as the Japanese, so they usually take a minute to cook it first. But *only* a minute, because it takes them the rest of the lunch hour to *pronounce* the lunch. For example, the Hawaiian word for triggerfish is *humuhumunukunukuapua'a*. (Don't even *ask* how they say 'lightly salted boiled soybeans.')

On the other hand, the Hawaiian word for fork is *'o*, which may help explain why cannibalism gained such a firm foothold in early Polynesian cultures. I mean, think about it. Here you are, an outsider from Europe, who hasn't bathed since Martin Luther bought a hammer. You sail into the harbor, wearing knickers and a pony-tail, and you're greeted by indigenous people who are starving to death because they can't pronounce humuhumunukunukuapua'a. They stare at you as they might stare at a glazed donut, if glazed donuts had been invented and wore knickers. The natives sway and bob a bit, and start asking around if anybody's got an *'o* handy. You don't know what *'o* means, so instead of racing back to the boat, you start handing out mirrors and rum.

But there you go. That's island life for you. Of course, you can't take your cultural cues from the Hawaiians.

After all, they whacked Captain Kangaroo.

Tonight's Specials

~*~*~

"He that but looketh on a plate of ham and eggs to lust after it hath already committed breakfast in his heart."

C.S. Lewis

~ *~*

"The one thing more exasperating than a wife who can cook and won't, is a wife who can't cook and will."

Robert Frost

Martha Gets a Restraining Order

Stalking. It's a good thing.

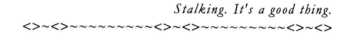

I should've known better.

Yeah, yeah, yeah. Hindsight, 20-20, blah blah blah. What was I thinking? Even in a relatively safe, anesthetic, de-clawed dating environment like match.com - I should've known better than to give Martha Stewart my phone number.

And now I can't get rid of her.

I'd already mentioned to some of you that I'd been thinking about dating again, for the same reasons as anybody else:

- I'd like to find a compatible, life-long partner, with whom I could share life's triumphs, failures, and intimacies
- I'm tired of throwing away food I can't finish
- I don't want to go to my grave not knowing what "chintz' is

81

- After a half-century of being completely free to do, eat, wear, and say whatever I want, whenever I want, I've finally run out of things to want

But when it comes down to actually wading into the dating pool, there are several things standing in my way:

- I want to meet women, but I don't want to leave my house
- In almost every instance, going out in public involves the hassle of putting on clothes
- After a week-load of dealing with corporate America, by the time Friday sails in, I'm ready to stab most people with a pencil

And that's a *real* 'inconvenient truth.' After years of working from home, and decades of full-time single-osity, I've grown very jealous of my weekends. Come Friday, I just want to turn off the phone, cook something angry, kick back, and listen to some Ella. Or Cat Stevens. (...the *old* Cat Stevens. The 'pre-Yusef' Cat Stevens. You know, back when he was a heathen.)

As some of you will remember, when my urge to mingle initially surfaced, I got over it pretty quickly, thanks to an unsettling story in the news about a date gone wrong. It involved a couple whose ill-fated romance had all the magical elements of a violin-drenched fairy tale: boy meets girl, boy mistreats girl, girl turns into Kathy Bates, attorney empanels jury for drawn-out murder trial.

No thanks. Dating, maybe. Dinner and a movie, sure. Death, blind rage, and boiled rabbits, I don't need.

But then, something utterly unforeseen happened. The world of online dating got a high-profile endorsement: Martha Stewart.

Yes, *the* Martha Stewart. The Handicraft Diva. The inept insider trading ingénue. Martha Stewart: media mogulette, former K-Mart towel pusher, current ex-con.

Here's a snip from her match.com profile:

"I'm told that I'm a specific person, and that the efficiency of online dating might be a good way for me to find that needle in a haystack."

Now that's a soul-stirring romantic right there. Pure poetry.

WANTED: Male needle. Must conform to my specific efficiencies. Should appreciate normal suburban hobbies, like installing swappable roof shingles in a variety of designer colors, or making a free-range artisan lasagna out of two odd-sized shoelaces and a Greek Orthodox ferret.

Ooh. I get chills.

This could be fun, I thought. Martha Stewart may have investment issues - and some fairly nasty ferret cookware - but as far as I know, she's never gone Lizzie Borden on anybody.

And I felt even more comfortable with that additional buffer online dating provides. I mean, what could go wrong, right? I could always pull back, or cancel the account, or say I was busy, or lie and claim to have contracted some violent disease that involves forehead blisters and outbreaks of insisting on separate checks.

And, after all, *this was Martha Stewart*. It's very likely I wouldn't have to worry about the normal irritants that are the standard curse and currency of online social media:

- People who substitute the number 2 for the word 'too,' the letter 'r' for the word 'are,' and are pathologically incapable of typing a sentence fragment without tacking on the acronym 'LOL'
- People who post completely bogus photos, or lie about their age, or otherwise misrepresent minor details about themselves; you know: name ... gender .. extended exposure to radioactivity ... a tendency to collect ferrets ... priors.
- @People who R #2hip 4 #thisgalaxy and type 2 @eachother N some Rcane, @stream-of-consciousness 4m of #moronspeak
- Three words: vegetarian lesbian vampires

So I gave it a try. And, for a while, things between Martha and me went swimmingly. Everything was nice and low-key, Martha was behaving, and I learned six ways to spruce up a prison cell with some infirmary toe tags, a few shivs, and a discarded carton of Luckies.

You Gonna Finish That Dragon?

But then, trouble.

Martha started getting pushy.

I don't know how or why it happened. It's not like I'm some great catch. Maybe she's just used to getting what she wants from a sycophantic staff of scarf-wearing eunuchs named Angelo and Thad. Maybe she'd figured on just making her own Mr. Right, in-between commercial breaks, from a discarded hay baler, two acorn squash, and a 'Fab' insert of Johnny Depp.

Or maybe it's because she's 71, and she senses the throb of that biological clock. (Of course, if she's 71 and eager for little feet pitter-pattering, she better tweak her 'the man for me' settings at match.com to channel Strom Thurmond.)

But however it happened, she suddenly started dropping little hints. Little conjugal hints.

Big trouble. The good ship Martha yawed hard toward Port Connubial.

Suddenly, I was ducking incoming questions like these:

- Honey, what do you think about the name 'Regis?'
- Just for the sake of argument, let's say you were planning a wedding reception ... you know, just hypothetically ... and let's say the decorating theme was "Victimized Indigenous Peoples of Our Dwindling Rain Forests." For the guest table centerpieces, would you rather have Brazilian or Peruvian scented pine needles?

- Where did *your* parents and their driver and personal kitchen staff go for their honeymoon?

And that's why I changed my online name to Bea Arthur.

Facebook's Timeline (for Dummies)

Now this is something new: software that hates you back
<>~<>~~~~~~~~~~<>~<>~~~~~~~~~~<>~<>

It's Tuesday, about 10am, and in case you hadn't noticed, facebook has changed its look-and-feel again. Seriously. Again. That's the third time they've reworked themselves this week. And it's only Tuesday, about 10am.

Facebook is the only website on Earth that's rendered in pencil.

This week's new version of the facebook interface is being marketed as the "Timeline," because "Timeline" sounds futuristic and hip, and because "Irritating Piece of Junk" was already taken.

Now, we're not here to pass judgment on facebook; after all, there are now an estimated 700 million facebook subscribers, as of Tuesday, about 10am. To put that in perspective, if facebook was a country, it would be the third largest country on the planet, and Ron Paul would be demanding that we get our troops out of facebook.

Over 700 million subscribers. That's a staggering success story, not to mention the potential religious implications of 700 million people all typing OMG at the same time.

So, before the next facebook makeover (scheduled for Tuesday, about 11am), let's review some of the new features of Timeline!

Timeline is a way to let you share your entire life's story online, by posting an embarrassing amount of personal information on a non-secure website that's potentially available to more bipeds than are listed in Madonna's rolodex.

The genius underpinning Timeline can be encapsulated by reviewing this list of Timeline's design goals:

- Analyze which features users like, and then hide them
- Analyze which menus users like, and then rename them (if it's a Friday, or an HR-designated "Marquis de Sade Day," remove the menus entirely)
- Randomly shuffle sections of the user's profile page so the sections show up in rude, nonsensical locations (including entirely different websites, or universes)

Timeline now allows you to customize your facebook page based on what type of facebook user you are. Most facebook users fall into one of these categories:

- The Steno: Champion of the sentence fragment, which is sometimes no more than just an acronym, like LOL, OMG, TMI or ROTFLMAO. The Steno hasn't composed a complete sentence since the second grade. (the sentence was "Feed me.") Probably works in network television advertising, or toxic waste management, which is redundant. IMHO.

- Captain Lockjaw: This is the guy who finds it impossible to complete a train of thought without tacking on a little smiley face caboose. Without the smiley face, Captain Lockjaw can't say anything, or reply to anything, or perform internal bodily functions like generating enzymes.

- The Poster Child: Never offers any actual syllables, but just spends all day forwarding giant images of family, forest animals, pets, blurred office parties, or witty, trenchant quips and bromides like "There is No I in Team" and "I Heart Vampire Topiary."

- Rasputin (aka, The Lurker): This is the mysterious, mute friend who never makes himself known. Never says a word. Never posts, never replies. Just...lurks. You know he's there, watching...waiting. Rasputin's like an ex-girlfriend that wants her albums back.

- Debbie Detritus: Debbie is that friend who invites you to events like the Obese Toenail Festival (next weekend in Rancid Gutter, Oklahoma). Debbie also sends you things...things that make you want to send Debbie to a very strict Spanish Inquisition revival: Debbie has sent you a Yak Cookie! Debbie has sent you a Timothy Leary Cocktail! Debbie wants you to have a Beaver Gland Corsage Inhaler!

- The Shrieker: TWO WORDS - CAPS LOCK

- The Exclaimer!: You love 'em!! Or you hate 'em!!!! But you can always gauge the intensity of their excitement, agreement, or anger by counting the number of exclamation marks they use!!!!!

- The Adam Sandler Trump Card: This friend can't help himself. He must reply to every comment, and he thinks his replies are hilarious. It's because of people like this that mankind invented euthanasia.

- The Reality Show Star: You know this one, too well. "I'm dropping little Tad off at soccer practice!" "I have to go to work!" "I'm on the way to work!" "I'm about to have some soup! Yum!" "I'm almost at work!" "My organs are generating enzymes! LOL!" "I'm growing faint from an internal hemorrhage! LOL!"

- The Giver: Here's that friend who says nothing, but shares everything. The Giver hasn't had an original thought since naming their first pet (Spot). It makes you wonder if they even *own* a keyboard.

- Bouncy Betty: Betty demands that you "like" something she saw because it's just the cutest thing you ever saw in your whole life! (Betty is closely related to The Exclaimer!)

- The Followers of Saint Biden: This is the group that can't string six words together without cursing. They're also known for their ability to turn any conversation into a double entendre: if someone comments, "I read where Eleanor Roosevelt once paved her driveway," a Follower will snort and toss back, "Yeah, I'd like to pave her driveway."

- The Free Thinkre: This free spirit believes they exist on a plane beyond literacy, and that spelling, grammar and punctuation are too Victorian for social media.

You Gonna Finish That Dragon?

They likely stare into the sky a lot and wear loose-fitting clothes. For the record, may I say this about the Free Thinkres: there wrong

Security, of course, is paramount in Timeline, and by paramount we mean insanely complicated. To take full advantage of the new security settings, follow these easy steps:

- Click "About"
- Curse mildly, then click "About" again, because while you were clicking "About" the first time, Timeline updated your status
- Click "My Secure Stuff"
- Buy two Farmville un-hatched yak egg coupon biscuits from the Mafia dwarf, after you've unlocked the Level Two cabbage dragon formerly held captive by the Deviated Septum of Ortho.
- Click "My Yak Yolk"
- Mop up the yak yolk with the dwarf
- Click "My Secure Stuff" again
- Choose "Encrypt Me"
- Facebook will generate a security code, which you should remember
- Log out and log back in
- Click "y-May ecure-Say uff-Stay"
- Enter your security code, which you forgot
- Choose who can access your medical records, your banking information, and your fully-mapped genome
- Click "Save"

- Curse mildly, because your Timeline session has timed out
- See Step 1

Alternatively, here's a little "geek insider" secret; a fun way to take full advantage of the tightest facebook security possible:

- Click "About"
- Take note of all that highly personal information of yours, that's potentially available to over 700 million people (as of 10am)
- Google the customer support phone number for facebook
- Call the number
- Unsubscribe

Anyway, we hope this little primer helps, and we just *know* you'll enjoy the new Timeline!

If you hurry.

Alas, Poor Sponge Cake!

Some times call for respect. This is not one of those times.
<>~<>~~~~~~~~~~<>~<>~~~~~~~~~~~<>~<>

It's a sad day, for those of us who eat.

By now, I suppose you've heard the bad news from the culinary world. No, not the news that Paula Deen will do her live holiday cooking special wearing spandex. The *other* bad news.

The Twinkie is dead. RIP, old friend.

Of course, as bad as this "no more Twinkies" news is for humans, it's even worse news for other species: I mean, in a Twinkie-free post-apocalypse, what are the cockroaches supposed to eat?

Personally, I haven't had a Twinkie in years, because my doctor won't let me - something to do with one of those numbers she's always measuring: high heart sugar, or low systolic resale value, or some such. She doesn't like it when I do risky things like have fun, or die, or anything else that might cause her to miss a boat payment.

93

But even though Twinkie and I haven't stayed in touch over the years, when Twinkie finally went to the Sweets By and By, I thought it deserved a little attention. After all, it's not that often that a post-apocalyptic sponge cake dies.

And that's when I learned, among many other things, that the Twinkie was invented by a man named James Dewar.

Dewar? Hmm.

I knew that name from my *own* (ancient) history as a bartender, though I'm not involved in that world anymore. Drinking always seems to make people do stupid stuff, like yell at furniture, or date.

So I kept digging, and suddenly Dewars started popping up everywhere. Then, as often happens, the weave of history started getting interesting. Here, I'll show you what I mean:

~-~-~-~-~-~

1805
John Dewar, the man who would eventually create the iconic Dewar's Scotch, was born in central Scotland to humble crofter parents (*'crofter'* is an ancient Gaelic term meaning *'I have more croft than you do'*). In fact, John's parents were *so* humble they couldn't afford to get John a middle name - they had to put it on layaway over at *Kilts 'R' Us.* (*'layaway'* is an ancient Gaelic term meaning *'well, we don't have THAT much croft'*)

1842

You Gonna Finish That Dragon?

Nearly forty years after John Dewar's birth, one James Dewar was born in Kincardine, Scotland, proving that middle names were still a luxury.

1851

In Adams Center, New York, Melville 'Melvil' Louis Kossuth Dewar was born with way more middle names than a man of his height would ever need. Melvil would go on to invent the Dewar Decimal System, which was a type of anal-retentive Rolodex file, except it kept track of books instead of normal stuff, like pizza delivery numbers, or ex-girlfriends.

(As you've probably figured out, Melvil wasn't really named 'Dewar.' Melvil's real surname was 'Dewey,' but if you're gonna niggle, we'll never get through this, so please settle down.)

(Plus, I got ten bucks that says you'll never again in your life see the name 'Melvil' used in five consecutive sentences.)

(You're welcome.)

1867

James Dewar, now an up-and-coming chemist, describes a few chemical formulae for benzene. Then he describes several more. Future parents, take note - this is the kind of ugly thing that can happen when you start skimping on middle names.

1880

John Dewar dies at age 74. Tragically, his parents had just one payment left on his middle name. (They had chosen 'Ethel', which would've been doubly tragic.) In his will, John bequeaths the family whiskey business to his sons, John Alexander Dewar and Thomas 'Tommy' Dewar. (along with that respectable middle name for John, and a nice set of single quotes for Tommy)

1886

Dewar's Scotch Whiskey wins its first medal. This was back when drinking Scotch was an Olympic sport. But back then, men also wore skirts and threw logs. Coincidence? Hmm.

(To complete their 19th-Century ensemble, men also played a confused wind instrument called a bagpipe, a thing that makes a noise like an oxygen-deprived yak with a deviated septum that got its tail caught in an escalator.)

1891

Dewar's Scotch makes its debut in Washington, DC. After a particularly painful and extended evening of toasts, log throwing, and barked shins, President Benjamin Harrison has electricity installed in the White House.

1892

Back in Scotland, James Dewar invents the flask. This was way better than just lapping up Scotch out of your cupped hands; plus, it led directly to the invention of the football stadium.

1897

Tommy 'Tommy' Dewar is appointed Sheriff of London, prompting William Shakespeare to coin the word 'graft,' which was an outstanding achievement for a 300-year-old dead guy. Tommy 'Tommy' went on to become Mayor of Chicago. And Governor of Illinois. And a State Senator. All at the same time.

Meanwhile, in Cook County, Illinois, James Alexander 'Hostess' Dewar was born. This is the Dewar who would eventually create the Twinkie. In keeping with Cook County custom, a local community organizer (Thaddeus Hubert Obama) immediately registered young Dewar to vote. As a Democrat. Twice.

1902

Tommy 'Tommy' Dewar is knighted, which was pretty outrageous, even for Chicago.

1904

A guy named 'Thermos' creates the ... well, duh. James 'Flask' Dewar sues Thermos for royalties, residuals and any future movie options. Dewar lost the case, however, when he fails to find his flask patent, possibly due to the fact that, benzene formulae notwithstanding, there was still no electricity.

1917

The Dewar's distillery in Aberfeldy is closed due to a war-time shortage of barley. This was before anybody had invented bullets, so soldiers would just lob various wheat products at each other.

1930 or 1931, depending on who you ask

The Twinkie is invented by the appropriate Dewar, I forget which already. Dewar, a suburban Chicago baker who made strawberry shortcakes, was looking for something to do in the off-season, when all the strawberries would go to Florida for the winter. So he filled his shortcakes with banana cream, as would any clear-thinking half-frozen baker. And the Twinkie was born.

According to Twinkie legend, Dewar came up with the name 'Twinkie' after seeing a Saint Louis billboard for 'Twinkle Toe Shoes,' which makes me think there were other Dewar's products involved, if you catch my drift.

1933
Prohibition ends in America. In Chicago, alcohol sales plummet. After all, it's no fun if it's legal.

1942
You're not gonna believe this, but Dewar's Aberfeldy Distillery had to close, again, due, again, to a war using up all the available barley.
Meanwhile, the Hostess Twinkie makers had to switch to a vanilla cream filling, due to ... ready? ... a war-time shortage of bananas.

And we wonder why Earth never gets contacted from outer space.

1972
The Twinkie Dewar retires. Hostess nicknames him "Mr. Twinkie," leaving the poor guy with no choice but to move to California, take up costume design, and avoid bars in Texas.

2000
President Bill Clinton puts a Twinkie in the millennial time capsule.

Before the capsule can be sealed, Newt Gingrich eats the Twinkie.

You Gonna Finish That Dragon?

Bill Clinton pardons Newt Gingrich.

~-~-~-~-~-~

See what I mean? Odd, isn't it? History can get so incredibly interwoven sometimes, especially when you're making up most of it.

And now Twinkie is gone. But maybe that's for the best. If you ever did a quick scan of Twinkie's ingredients, it can be a bit sobering (Pun intended. Sorry, relevant Dewars). Besides the normal polysyllabic list of chemicals and carcinogens, each Twinkie contains ... ready? ... beef fat.

It gets better.

A Twinkie also contains something that its producers will only list as 'solids.'

Solids. Mmm.

"Hey, Mom! Any more solids?"
"Not until you finish all your benzene."

Maybe that's why the lovely little sponge cakes have that legendary reputation that they're gonna last forever.

Or at least until the next Barley Wars.

Barry Parham

Abby Redux IX

Our favorite grumpy advice columnist takes on facebook and other bacteria

<>~<>~~~~~~~~~~<>~<>~~~~~~~~~~~<>~<>

Well, I did it. It took some effort; after all, she's pretty busy these days, and she doesn't think much of me. (For that matter, she doesn't think much of you, either. Or you.) But I did it.

Abby's back.

For those of you who haven't met her, Abby Redux is an advice columnist who pops round every now and again to share her column with us. Abby has several interesting characteristics:

1. She has the same first name as another famous advice columnist and the same last name as a famous John Updike novel
2. She has a seriously bad attitude and no patience whatsoever, which, you have to admit, is an intriguing approach for an advice columnist
3. She doesn't actually exist

Some say Abby should work on her interpersonal skills - a tricky challenge at best, what with her being all, like, nonexistent and stuff. Others maintain that, given the caliber of questions lobbed at her, we're lucky she's not facing multiple indictments for felony assault.

I'll let you decide.

~-~-~-~-~-~

Dear Abby Redux,
Today on facebook, I saw a profile of a young man who said he was a woman. Then he/she said she/he was in a relationship. With another woman. I'm very confused.
Signed, Dotty Frump

Dear Dotty,
This is why our parents always told us to go the bathroom *before* getting in the car.
~-~-~-~-~-~

Dear Abby Redux,
Remember those nuclear reactors in Japan that were damaged by earthquakes and tsunamis? Did you hear the Japanese government has decided it's safe to turn them back on?
Signed, Rhett Allurt

Dear Rhett,
I wouldn't worry about it. Hey - damaged nuclear reactors, tsunamis, Pacific Ring of Fire, Godzilla - what could go wrong?
But if I were you, I'd stock up on canned tuna.

~-~-~-~-~-~-~

Dear Abby Redux,
Looks like the election season's reached the next phase. Somebody on the news said that Mitt Romney is spending the next few days on a bus tour.
Signed, Paul Stuhr

Dear Paul,
Must be an awfully big bus.

~-~-~-~-~-~-~

Dear Abby Redux,
Looks like the election season's reached the next phase. The President keeps showing up on TV, saying illegal aliens are American citizens in every way except one: "on paper." What's that mean, *on paper?* What is he talking about?
Signed, Eileen Wright

Dear Eileen,
Let's put it this way. Go to a car dealership, find a car you like, and take it home. Just drive it off the lot and keep it. Later, when the TV crews and the SWAT team converge on your lawn, just tell 'em you own the car in every way except one.
And good luck in prison.

~-~-~-~-~-~-~

Dear Abby Redux,
The guys at work invited me to join them for lunch. But the place they chose was a strip-tease/pole-dancing club that has, if you can believe it, a lunch buffet. Do you think I should accept the invite? I don't want to seem rude.

Signed, Maury Gretz

Dear Maury,
Go, go. Enjoy the buffet. Just avoid the food. And if your waitress is wearing a sneeze guard, run like the wind.
~-~-~-~-~-~

Dear Abby Redux,
Y'all gone love this. My old lady drove over by the Kwik Korner Mart to grab some beer, cigarettes, bait, and this month's edition of *Popular Quantum Mechanics*. Then, I reckon, the cashier punched up some buttons wrong.
Haaaaw! Was the wife ever whiffed when the cash register displayed a total of $18,228! Why, it narrilly got ugly!
Signed, Parvo N. Sutch

Dear Parvo,
Eighteen large? Filled up with gas, too, did she?
~-~-~-~-~-~

Dear Abby Redux,
On facebook, I keep seeing profiles of young men wearing lots of eye makeup, and girls of an impressionable age sporting shaved heads, lizard tattoos, and full combat gear. Their faces all look like they were attacked by shiny napkin rings. It's all very confusing. How many genders do we have now anyway?
Signed, Dotty Frump

Dear Dotty,
You might wanna give facebook a few days' rest. Concerning your 'how many genders' question; well, that depends. On the

East Coast, we're still going with two. On the West Coast, the jury's still out.

~-~-~-~-~-~

Dear Abby Redux,
I heard that the British Prime Minister left one of his children in a bar. Is the kid okay?
Signed, Roy L. Gokker

Dear Roy,
The kid's fine. As it happens, that pub was a scheduled stop on Mitt Romney's bus tour. He untied his dog from the top of the bus, strapped on little Britlet, and safely got the lad home. But Romney, in turn, forgot the dog at the bar.
Unfortunately, the same bar had been targeted by Michelle Obama's "Schooner or Later Tour," her whirlwind crusade to have draft beer replaced by a low-sodium vegetable medley. And at some point during the afternoon's occupation of the pub, President Obama ate the dog.

~-~-~-~-~-~

Dear Abby Redux,
Here in South Carolina, a woman was accused of forging checks and then stealing over $100,000 in stuff from Home Depot. What an idiot! Didn't even check the Lowe's across the street for better prices!
Signed, Ida Shoptmore

Dear Ida,
It gets better. The forger was assisted by a newly hired clerk, an orange-vested octogenarian named Maury Gretz. Imagine Lady Forger's conversation with *that* guy:

~_~_~_~_~_~

Maury: Hi. Thanks for choosing Home Depot, which you didn't have to do, since for some insane reason we're always located directly across the street from a Lowe's. My name's Maury, and I'm the only person in my family to have nearly completed the fourth grade.

Forger: Who are all those people lined up out front?

Maury: Illegal aliens.

Forger: Can we still say 'illegal aliens?'

Maury: Sorry. Undocumented Democrats.

Forger: What are they doing out front?

Maury: Contractors drive up, the day-workers hop in, contractors drive off. It's kinda like a makeshift employment office, but without that pesky "taxable wages" angle.

Forger: Ah. Hey, I'd like to buy all these stoves.

Maury: OK.

Forger: Do you have any more?

Maury: Yes.

Forger: Do you have any more?

You Gonna Finish That Dragon?

Maury: Yes.

Forger: Do you have any more?

Maury: No.

Forger: Can I buy some illegal aliens?

Maury: I'll have to ask.

~-~-~-~-~-~

Dear Abby Redux,
OMG. My BFF read a facebook post that said Hawaiian natives used to kill sharks by boiling coconuts and then throwing the boiling hot coconuts at the sharks!
Signed, Hannah Lou Lewe

Dear Hannah,
And some still say there's no scientific proof for global warming.

~-~-~-~-~-~

Dear Abby Redux,
My doctor just switched one of my meds, and it's causing some unexpected side effects. I find myself madly attracted to any man dressed like Thor, the god of thunder. What do you advise?
Signed, Tia Neigh

Dear Tia,
I just ran your question by the guys on my staff, and they asked me to ask you: what's the name of that medication?

~-~-~-~-~-~

Dear Abby Redux,
Did you see that amazing video of the tightrope walker? The one who walked across Niagara Falls from Canada to America? Wow!
Signed, Esa Lee Amuste

Dear Esa,
It gets better. Now that they guy got across the border in to America, he's instantly eligible for health care, in-state tuition, and provisional membership in the Elks. Afterwards, he'll be driven by an ACORN staffer to either a voter registration office or an abortion clinic.
Then, in return for registering as a Democrat voter, he'll get to have dinner with the President, both Arlen Specters, and either Sarah Jessica Parker or Seabiscuit.
Of course, depending on the cognitive and observational skills of our new friend, he may realize that, technically, he can't have an abortion because he's not a she. Not a problem! Planned Parenthood will take care of the sex change operation, arrange for him to get pregnant, take care of the abortion and all the paperwork and, for a small fee, set up His and Her facebook accounts.

Dotty's gonna *love* that.
~-~-~-~-~-~

Dear Abby Redux,
Maybe you can verify this for me. Somebody on facebook said one of the fast food chains is gonna add bacon sundaes to their menu! Can you imagine such a thing?

You Gonna Finish That Dragon?

Signed, Anna Richsia

Dear Anna,

Wouldn't surprise me at all. Apparently that tired, boring health food craze has died of malnutrition. I heard that Dairy King will soon be offering drive-thru cholesterol injections, and Burger Queen is test marketing something they call the Triple Blockage With Cheese. The Hard Rock Café is looking to debut a "Kevin Bacon Burger" that *actually includes* Kevin Bacon.

Next thing you know, we'll be seeing "I Dare You To Eat All This" ads from Five EMT Guys, Jack-in-the-Pine-Box, and Taco Knell.

~-~-~-~-~-~

Dear Abby Redux,

I'm at my wit's end. My husband got on facebook and fell in love with my therapist's ex-husband. What do I do?

Signed, Senator Clyde Stale

Dear Senator,

Can't talk to you right now, dear. I've a bit of an office emergency. All my staff just showed up dressed as Norse gods.

~-~-~-~-~-~

Dear Abby Redux,

On facebook, I got a friend request from a group of Vegan Cambodian Transgendered Vampire Nudist Bikers. They're trying to raise money to stage some kind of "Four Horsemen" protest near a nuclear reactor somewhere in Japan. Should I accept the friend request?

Signed, Dotty Frump

Dear Dotty,
Shut up.
~-~-~-~-~-~-~

The High Cost of Free Stuff

facebook: a quick surreality check

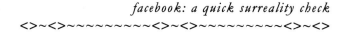

Well, here we are in early December. A nice calm in-between cacophonies. The national elections are behind us. The Thanksgiving traffic is behind us. Black Friday and Cyber Monday are behind us. But some real, serious stupidity is on the horizon. So while we have a minute, let's talk about something that's not insultingly stupid.

Like facebook.

Yeah, good point. Okay, let's talk about something *different.*

facebook: that thing we love to hate. facebook has become the Archie Bunker of the digital generation: strange, loud, and full of crude remarks - but still oddly addictive; not really dangerous, but not really helpful, either; opinionated, but ultimately irrelevant.

facebook is a lot like the way *The Hitchhiker's Guide to the Galaxy's* famous *Encyclopedia Galactica* describes Earth: mostly harmless.

111

You can tell that facebook has reached an iconic level in American culture, because our elder saints - the members of the *real* Greatest Generation - are officially "worried about" facebook. And you can tell they're officially worried because they've started adding that dreaded code-word for "trouble ahead" - the prefacing "the." You know the "the" I mean:

"My daughter spends all her time on the facebook."

"That bar's got the rock-n-roll. Shameful."

"I hope he's not doing the marijuana."

"Cheez, these Commies!"
"Archie, are you on the facebook?"
"Stifle."

According to the internet, there are now over 1 billion facebook users, possibly as many as six of them using their real name. A billion people. Imagine that. One out of every seven people on Earth, steadily misusing "they're" and "its," overusing exclamation points, and reflexively typing "lol" every eleven seconds.

One out of seven. It's weird. Why, if you randomly picked any 100 people on Earth, chances are they would be *more effective than the current US Senate.* (No, that's *not* relevant to this discussion, but it's still pretty weird.)

And believe me: these facebook fan(atic)s - I call them "the SocNets" - take their facebook very seriously. If a SocNet reads something on facebook, it is Truth (or as the SocNets would put it, it is "like wholly writ and stuff lol.")

So, as a public service to the SocNets - and at the risk of being a stormcrow - here's a partial list of clarifications lol:

- Not everyone wants to play Farmville. Really. They don't.
- There is no miracle fruit that is 10,000 times more effective than chemotherapy.
- Abraham Lincoln does not, in fact, have his own facebook page.
- No. Seriously, no. They don't want to play Farmville. Or Farmville 2. Stop asking.
- No, they don't want to play Pet Society or Pet Rescue Saga or Fishville, either.
- There is not some kind of mystical connection between facebook and the universe, comingling in such a way that if you share a certain post with a certain number of SocNets within a certain period of time, good things will happen to you. What is more likely is that all those SocNet share-ees will start lol-ing @ u.
- Warnings from "friends" to ignore messages from this-person-or-that will not cause your computer to become infected with a virus. Remember: these "friends" are people who can no longer complete a sentence without lobbing in an "lol," an acronym which has now officially become the most-typed phrase since the English language was invented in the Fifth Century by Cedric "Al" Gorewulf. (*source: Wicked-Step-Ex-Pedia*)

- No, not even Mafia Wars. Or Lost Bubble, Bubble Blitz, Bubble Epic, or Yoville, either. Really, they don't.

- The universal wisdom contained in a facebook post is not directly proportional to the number of exclamation points used to punch up that post.

- If you've sent someone five thousand invitations to play games, and they've pleaded with you to stop sending them game invitations, you will not wear them down by sending them several thousand more.

- Clicking "like" on a photoshopped picture of an allegedly health-challenged human (or animal) will not automagically generate a cash donation to that human/imal's health situation.

- You cannot modify facebook's rules, guidelines, privacy policies, mission statement, or internal genetic structure simply by posting some bobo cheesy quasi-legal disclaimer, even if said disclaimer includes Perry Mason-ish terms like "heretofore" or "therein" or "Berner Convention."

- You cannot get a computer virus simply by adding this-person-or-that as a "friend." On the other hand, should you choose to meet that person late one night for a friendly cocktail at some dim back-street bar named "Selma's House of Pain" without even confirming that this new "friend" is the gender they say they are, all bets are off.

- By the way: there is no such thing as a "Berner Convention."

- It is not true that people just can't get enough of photos of cats posing anthropomorphically above captions of mangled, misspelled baby talk.

- Regardless of the actual exclamation point tonnage, the rest of us do not, in fact, *"have to see this!!!"* Neither is it likely to be *"the best thing ever!!!"* nor is it guaranteed to *"leave"* us in *"tears!!!"* But if you keep it up, there's a *"good chance"* we will *"never contact you again."*

- When calculating your credit score, the major credit bureaus no not take into account the number of "friends" you have on facebook. However, the bureaus may consider the number of "friends" you have named "Sybil the Trisexual Vegan Vampire," or if your résumé lists the Berner Convention as a former employer.

- There is no app that can tell you who has recently viewed your profile. The fact that you are that desperately interested in your own profile is kinda scary.

- LOL is still an acronym for "Laughing Out Loud." It is not short for "Lucifer Our Lord." However, if your profile name is "Sybil the Trisexual Vegan Vampire," all bets are off.

- No matter how many "friends" you have on facebook, very, very few of them care that you just scored a Double Taupe Glazed Ferret Discount Yo-Bonus in Mafia Farmville Bingoland Sim-Wars III.

- If all you ever do is share other people's posts, you are not providing the online world with a valuable and otherwise neglected service. At least once every 4-6 months, try to have an original thought.

- When someone asks you to "post this on your status for one hour," and you don't do it, that does not mean you don't like that person. However, if they keep doing that, you may soon learn to dislike them. A lot.

- By the way: that same person may say they know, in advance, which of their friends will post it. No, they don't.

- They may also quote some percentage ("78.298% of you won't post this on your status for one hour"), claiming they know this percentage to be true.

- No, they don't.

- If they challenge your facts, threaten to bring them before the Berner Convention.

- God is not going to decide how you spend eternity based on whether or not you share a post.

- If you have enough common sense not to click on links that promise you free iPhones, then be happy. You are smarter than 78.298% of SocNets.

And one more thing.

- On the pending Mayan doomsday this December, facebook is not planning to automatically start dragging the Earth into the Sun.

- This is not an option that you can change by going to Settings > Planetary Settings > Trajectory.

- And there is no 'Avoid Apocalypse' checkbox that you can tick.

I hope that helped clear up some misconceptions. We're at a nice, calm pause in the year just now, and we don't need any distractions. After all, it's December, and you know what that means. You know what's coming.

No, not "last call" at Club Maya. Worse.

Burl Ives.

iNertia, v2.0

Lazy? There's an app for that.

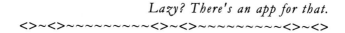

As a career single guy, I'm constantly on the lookout for time-saving devices, as long as the looking doesn't take too much effort.

"But Barry," you may say, "time-saving devices are for lazy people, not single guys." And I may reply, after I run several hundred yards away because I don't really know you and I have no idea how gracefully you handle confrontation, "Shut up." (I'll reply loudly, so you can hear me.)

See, being lazy and being a single guy are really just two ways of saying the same thing. And, being lazy, I'm rarely *ever* tempted to say the same thing twice. Heck, sometimes I need a coffee infusion, or some vague, looming threat of pending physical violence, before I'll bother saying something *once*.

And as mentioned, I'm 'career' lazy. I'm lazy like somebody was handing out prizes...as if there was some International Sloth Awareness awards committee, who finally had to ask me to stay home this year and give somebody else a chance.

119

But other than the ISA judges, most people don't appreciate how much effort it takes to be inert.

Here's how lazy I am: recently, to save an entire minute a day, I quit shaving and just grew a beard. But then I spent more time *scratching* at my face than I'd *ever* spent scraping it. So, next, in a misguided effort to be lazy *and* cool, I went with a mustache and chin beard (also known as a 'goatee' or a 'Van Dyke' or, in traveling circus circles, 'Fatima the Geek Lady'). Basically, I was walking around in public, randomly frightening children, with the facial hair equivalent of a love child fathered by Colonel Sanders and Old Scratch.

That partial hair ploy turned out to be an even *more* idiotic idea on my part, because now, not only did I have to shave - I had to *not* shave, too. I had to shave in zones. I had to shave *and* stay in the lines. I had turned my head into a kindergarten coloring book, but without a graham cracker. Or a nap.

I'd shave my head entirely, but I'm too lazy to calculate the Band-Aid budget.

Career single guys are a breed apart. In more ways than you might imagine, single guys are different from people who have kids and other tax deductions. I've seen it. I've been to homes that house whole families. Family people are used to a residual level of background noise. In my house, if I hear a noise I didn't make, someone's breaking in.

And single guys jealously guard that privacy, that silence, that inertia. Single guys have even learned how to doze without interruption while watching FoxNews, a network that has adopted the marketing technique of screaming "BREAKING NEWS" every time a plane crashes, or doesn't crash, or lands, or takes off, or taxis, or boards, or is on time, or is delayed, or gets bought, or sold, or cleaned.

However, don't confuse the single guy with his sociological cousin, the bachelor. Sure, on the surface, single guys and bachelors may seem the same:

1) No one is barking in their ear, "See? I told you, you should've turned left!"
2) No one is barking in their ear, "See? I told you about those socks!"
3) They're lost, and their socks don't match.

But internally, we're wired differently. Bachelors don't have *time* to be lazy, because bachelors are still 'on the market.' 'On the market' means bachelors who are still looking for women who are 'available,' because these bachelors still think themselves 'a good catch,' even though they are 'older than Methuselah' and are wearing 'purchased hair' and 'orthopedic socks.' All of this combines to make bachelors 'funny to watch,' not to mention 'stupid.'

To be fair, though, in some ways, we're a lot alike, too. Single guys and bachelors both leap for the television whenever some stiletto-sporting TV news hair helmet mentions that they're about to show "an info-graphic."

(It's not our fault. See, "Coming up, an info-graphic" sounds just like "Coming up, a nympho-graphic," especially if you're 'stupid' or you just dropped your hair.)

So, to revisit our original question: why bother saying 'single guy' *and* 'lazy'? It would be like saying you're a long-tailed cat *and* nervous, or saying you're in a Detroit auto union *and* drinking during lunch.

"But Barry," you may say, "if you're so lazy, why do you say 'single guy' when 'lazy' takes less time to say?" And, this time, I may not reply to you at all, because you've now entered Barking In My Ear Land, and I'll be too busy making sure I never invited you to my house by mistake.

But I'll answer your question anyway, since you asked, and since I need about 75 more words for this week's humor column so that I can submit it to both surviving American newspapers so the editors can reject it without bothering to comment. The reason I prefer to say 'single guy' instead of 'lazy' is rooted in my long-standing addiction to (and fascination with) one of the best board games of all time, Scrabble.

Scrabble puts a high premium on certain special letters, like Z, Q, and the inter-office correspondence of Dick Cheney. So I naturally respect things like the letter Z, and the letter Q, and Dick Cheney, especially during quail season.

(By the way, playing the word 'quail' in Scrabble is one of those life-changing victories that hits a single guy where it counts, like winning a beer lottery, or seeing an info-graphic.)

But this week I may have stumbled upon the absolute ultimate in lazy. Witness:

Somewhere out there, a proud author published his eBook, entitled *Progeny*, and (rightly) started firing off marketing efforts to help sell the book. I wish him nothing but the best of luck, of course. I wish him tons of sales. I wish him a spot on Oprah's speed dial. I wish him yachts, and I wish him cramps accrued from signing royalty checks, and I wish him a severely disorienting mental condition that leaves him convinced that I'm his sole heir.

However, among his promotional efforts, he bulk-blasted a marketing email, and here's how it read:

FREE PROGENY ON YOUR KINDLE!

Wow. Free, virtual kids.

Now *that's* lazy.

Barry Parham

My, Aren't You Not Looking Lovely!

Remember: if you can't say anything nice, you're probably a guy.

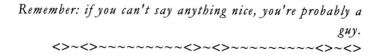

Okay, guys. Whoever's in charge of keeping the list this week: here's the latest *"don't"* -- never tell a woman she looks nice. Because you could end up in court.

And you thought *carpool lane* violations were harsh.

But it's true: a guy could now get sued for complimenting a female coworker. According to a story in the news, some poor putz has been "disciplined" at work - disciplined by HR Lady, that dreaded star of daymares - for daring to pay a lady a compliment.

True, sources say the putz paid the compliment while wearing a caveman costume, clown feet, and a Hannibal Lector mask. At a church. During a funeral. While reciting a limerick that delved into areas of biology not

125

generally championed at corporate seminars as "HR-approved." But still...c'mon. I mean, let's relax, people. Lighten up, Babe.

It *is* 'Babe,' isn't it?

[Legal Disclaimer: the proceeding comment was in no way intended to cast aspersions on women named 'Babe,' farm animals named 'Babe,' or women who look like farm animals. This also applies to California government employees who might choose at some future time, and at taxpayer expense, to become women.]

I remember a time when things were different. (But then, I remember a time when we had just two genders.) Once upon a time, children, men used to hold doors open for women. Seriously! When a woman and a man were entering a building, or a room in that building, the man would open the door, smile, and allow the woman to enter the room before him. Once upon a time, this type of behavior was called "manners." Now, it's known as "sexual harassment." What once was "being polite" is now a "pending lawsuit."

Long ago, back in the days before people entertained themselves (and others) by falling into mall fountains while texting, guys used to engage in another now-extinct social behavior: tipping the hat. It worked like this: a man, approaching a woman in public, would simply touch the brim of his hat. That's it! A gracious, non-threatening gesture that tacitly acknowledges two things:

1) You are a woman, and you deserve respect.
2) I am a man, and I don't trust myself to say anything, because the truth is I am never more than about two troglodyte genes away from clown feet and a limerick.

And then the man would walk on, at peace with his world and whistling a happy tune, before eventually falling into a mall fountain.

These were, admittedly, things belonging to a long-forgotten, dusty age, a time when the hat was an integral, proper part of a man's wardrobe, like sporting a nice silk tie, or wearing pants positioned at the same altitude as your waist.

[Legal Disclaimer: the proceeding comment was in no way intended to cast aspersions on men who put their pants only halfway on. Who knows - maybe their pants are *not*, in fact, on the ground! Maybe they have extremely long abdomens, or very short shins. Perhaps it's some obscure, butt-focused form of energy conservation. Perhaps these gentlemen have simply misinterpreted scripture; in particular, the *"lo"* part of *"and lo shall they be clothed."*]

But fashion's not the only thing that's changed. These days, a guy can get into big trouble just for pointing out that Susie is, to use the technical term, a straight-up hottie. Why, even our own President recently got tsk-tsked for pointing out that California's Attorney General was the "best-looking AG in the country."

Of course, the goal of "best-looking AG" isn't exactly setting a high bar. Attorneys General throughout history are rarely remembered for turning heads - you almost never seen any "Attorney General of the Month" pinup calendars, or any History Channel specials titled "Smokin' Hot AGs of the 1800s." In fact, a portrait of America's very first AG, one Edmund Randolph, presents a man with a nose that could house its own military base.

By the way: that AG gaffe wasn't the President's fault, of course; after all, he just reads what his keepers tell him to read. (And to be fair, members of Congress would do the exact same thing, too, if they could read.)

[Legal Disclaimer: for the record, our President is fully capable of performing other Presidential duties beyond reciting scripts from teleprompters. He can also putt.]

It's just one more sign of The End. Forget the Mayans. We don't need a 5,000-year-old pinup calendar to let us know that civilization has hopped a cosmic cab...especially a pinup calendar so heavy it would take industrial rivets to pin it to your locker.

You Gonna Finish That Dragon?

[Legal Disclaimer: the proceeding *'heavy'* analogy referred specifically to the ancient Mayan calendar's being made of stone. It was in no way intended to portray primordial pinup girls as overweight, or of being able to support military facilities. I'm sure that early Mesoamerican babes were very hot, in a savage, human-heart-eating kind of way, despite running around in turquoise lipstick and having names like Txlpotetecl.]

Here's one more on-topic anecdote, involving me acting my advanced age. One day, lately, I made the mistake of opening the passenger-side car door for a lady. (Guys used to do insensitive stuff like that all the time, children. But that was back before science discovered guys were full of diseases, with scary names like "baggage" and "angst.")

So, on that recent day, as a female coworker and I were leaving the office to attend a cross-town meeting, I had a fatal lapse, causing me to pop around to the passenger side of my car to open the door for the lady. But, you see, the lady wasn't used to this custom. All she saw was some aging guy with eyebrow dandruff, on the wrong side of the car in an unpatrolled parking lot, holding a car key and rapidly closing in.

I won't bore you with the gory details, except to say this: mace *hurts*.

Finally, just to try and maintain a balance about America's anti-compliment neurosis, let's head over to the other side of the world for a different perspective. Recently, in China, a man sued his wife for being ugly.

...and the court agreed.

Of course, what can you expect from a country whose secret agents are so inscrutably evil that they captured Kiefer Sutherland during sweeps week, locked him in a secret prison, and tortured him so severely that the next season's plots contained characters who, we know for a fact, died two seasons ago.

[Legal Disclaimer: the proceeding reference to Jack Bauer and evil Chinese agents was in no way intended to malign the great, peace-loving nation of China and their massive militar...Hang on, someone's at the door...]

Yes? Who are *you* guys?

No, I didn't order any Chinese food, Babe.

It *is* 'Babe,' isn't it?

Oww! What th...

No, wait! No, I didn't mean to offen...

Oww!

Look, it was just a humor colu...

No, I jus...

Oww!

Abby Redux X

Our grumpy columnist drops by, and soon regrets every
minute of it
<>~<>~~~~~~~~~<>~<>~~~~~~~~~~<>~<>

This week, I'm pleased to mumble a non-binding 'Welcome back!' to Abby Redux, everybody's favorite jaded advice columnist.

For the three of you out there who read my weekly humor columns (my Mom, my Dad, Eric Holder), Abby and her irregular advice column need no introduction. But if you're not familiar with her work, Abby Redux is one of many media confidantes who field questions and serve up life-coping counsel for people -- but with a twist: Abby doesn't *like* people.

Abby's been a bit low-profile over the last few months, in part due to a pesky "disagreement" that involves a moonstruck yoga instructor, a statute of limitations, and a petty, narrow definition of "automatic weapon."

But the news from America has gotten so bizarre lately that citizens are grasping for ways to deal with it all. The people want some honest analysis. The people need a straight-shooter.

And when it comes to shootin' straight, Abby is packin'.

Welcome back, Abby.
~-~-~-~-~-~-~

Dear Abby Redux,
What in the world's going on in the White House these days? Every time I turn on the TV, it's another scandal! It's like I'm watching reruns of *"Dynasty,"* but with a cast of ugly people.
Signed,
Doris From Dallas

Dear Doris,
Could be worse. At least we're not seeing plus-sized civil servants in dance videos.
Oh, wait.
~-~-~-~-~-~-~

Dear Abby Redux,
A friend of mine said he read somewhere that Obama's Attorney General, Eric Holder, told the truth once, in 1967. Can you confirm this?
Signed,
Bernie From Birmingham

Dear Bernie,
Not true. He nearly made a factual comment once, in 1985, a short-sighted action that almost hobbled his budding career as a Washington lawyer.

You Gonna Finish That Dragon?

In a story that's completely unrelated, but still funny somehow, Holder once represented Chiquita, where he acquitted several of their top bananas before they split. (The verdict was overturned on a peel.)

~-~-~-~-~-~

Dear Abby Redux,
Whatever happened to that woman who was on trial for accidently stabbing her boyfriend 50 times?
Signed,
Contemplating in Kalamazoo

Dear Contemplating,
The trial was delayed after the accused accidently shot the jury. She accidently shot them the next day, too. Twice.

~-~-~-~-~-~

Dear Abby Redux,
I heard on the news that the Senate is finally (!) dealing with some Border Security legislation. But already, after just the first draft, they've slapped on something like 300 pages of amendments. What's up with *that*?
Signed,
Ari Tsonah

Dear Ari,
They had to. In the Senate's original version of the Border Security bill, they forgot to mention one detail ... Border security.

~-~-~-~-~-~

Dear Abby Redux,

My friend said that Mark Sanford, South Carolina's disgraced, GPS-challenged ex-Governor, somehow managed to get SC voters to elect him to Congress ... *even after having to resign as Governor.* Is that true?
Signed,
A Non-Bitter Lady Named Myrtle

Dear Stephen Colbert's Therapist,
Yep. It's true. Kinda makes you wonder just how bad the *other* candidate was, huh? I'm guessing Sanford's opponent might've been that whackstick woman who accidently killed her boyfriend 50 times.

~-~-~-~-~-~

Dear Abby Redux,
I just wanted to publicly congratulate New Jersey's Governor, Chris Christie, on his plan to try and lose some weight. Speaking as someone who's currently under a restraining order from the lunch buffet at Ryan's, I appreciate his struggles.
Signed,
Vera O. Beese

Dear Vera,
Christie's drastic "lap band" weight-loss surgery suffered a setback today when the Governor ate the hospital's attending anesthesiologist.

~-~-~-~-~-~

Dear Abby Redux,
Recently, a Georgetown professor compared Eric Holder to Moses. What's even more weird, the same professor once

referred to Barack Obama as a Pharaoh. What next? Hillary Clinton as Edward G. Robinson?
Signed,
A Totally Non-Partisan Observer

Dear Newt,
Give Georgetown a break. They don't have time to run around micromanaging every little psychotic episode among the faculty; they're too busy fund-shopping for free condoms.

Besides...Seriously? Eric Holder as *Moses?* Right. Eric Holder couldn't part red *tape.*

And forget Hillary. She's just making an asp of herself.
~-~-~-~-~-~

Dear Abby Redux,
Whatever happened to that woman who, like, shot her boyfriend and stuff? I mean, like, after she stabbed him, like, 50 times and stuff. That's, like, a total life fail. As if.
Like, Signed,
Penumbra Neon Stamen

Dear Headed for a Career on the Pole,
Insider sources say Quentin Tarantino has offered to pony up for Barbiturate Barbie's bail, in return for movie rights. You should probably, like, give Quentin a call, too. And stuff.
~-~-~-~-~-~

Dear Abby Redux,
I just don't know America anymore. We have throttling debt, choking unemployment, and a gasping dollar. We have

scandals in the Justice Department, the Treasury Department, the State Department, the EPA, and the IRS. Due to political budget cuts, our military only get two meals a day, but military prisoners get three.

And what story leads in the mainstream media? New pictures of Barack Obama's high school prom.

I don't know anymore.
Signed,
Avuncular Sam

Dear Sam,
Welcome to Planet Lemming. We'd take you to our leader, but We. Don't. Have. One.
~-~-~-~-~-~

Dear Abby Redux,
I don't mean to niggle, but I must say I'm outraged at this Penny Pritzker, Obama's nomination for Commerce Secretary. Not only is she Obama's close friend, *and* one of his powerhouse fundraisers; she also failed to claim *eighty million dollars* of income! Eighty million! If I had that kind of money, I'd be a whole lot more responsible with it!
Signed,
Mollie Justed

Dear Mollie,
Responsible, schmonsible. If you had that kind of money, you'd be fighting off marriage proposals from John Kerry.
~-~-~-~-~-~

You Gonna Finish That Dragon?

Dear Abby Redux,

Here's a fun question that's going around on facebook: Julie's mom has five daughters. The first four are named Rana, Rene, Rini, and Rono. What is the name of the fifth daughter? LOL
Signed,
Irritating Social Media Troll

Dear Rachel Maddow,

The fifth daughter's name? Fred. It *was* Julie, but Julie moved to the West Coast, got a job with the city of Oakland, and received a taxpayer-funded sex change. Now Fred runs a pro-biotic, free range ferret Anger Management center. Fred will live happily ever after with her common law husband, Carla.
~_~_~_~_~_~

Dear Abby Redux,

Are you kidding me? The Attorney General, Eric Holder, is going to investigate himself?
Signed,
Duh

Dear Duh,

Fortunately, attorney Eric Holder was able to clear the defendant, Eric Holder, after Judge Eric Holder threw out the star witness, Eric Holder, resulting in a hung jury composed of twelve peers (all named Eric Holder).
~_~_~_~_~_~

Dear Abby Redux,

Wait till you hear this! The Governor of Florida is in a fight to outlaw the use of food stamps at casinos and strip clubs. Can you believe that's going on?

Signed,
A Jersey Businessman

Dear Mr. Trump,
I can just imagine the conversation at that betting window:
"Gimme a quart of milk, some Huggies, and a lap dance."
~_~_~_~_~_~

Dear Abby Redux,
Some goofball has done mailed more of that poison stuff, that Ricin, to President Barack America, and to that mayor fella up in New York City.
Signed,
Typical Semi-Literate Bigoted Ignorant White Male

Dear MSNBC Staff,
The White House is denying any knowledge of the story, but they're blaming two rogue part-time park rangers in the IRS's Nome, Alaska office.

The NYC package never made it to Bloomberg's office because the container was over 16 oz.
~_~_~_~_~_~

Dear Abby Redux,
Any update on that woman who committed first-degree self-defense?
Signed,
Charlene Manson

Dear Charl,

Last I heard, the anti-socialite had made judicial history, as the first defendant found "not guilty due to very high Nielsen ratings." After her release, she formed her own band (featuring Eric Holder on lead guitar, Senator Paul Simon as songwriter Paul Simon, and the IRS Dancers), and wowed the "American Idol" judges with a catchy tune, "50 Ways to Cleave Your Lover."

I'm getting too old for this.

~-~-~-~-~-~

Barry Parham

Mark's Twenty Billion New Friends

Insipid polls, intolerant vampires, and initial public offerings. What a great country!

<>~<>~~~~~~~~~~<>~<>~~~~~~~~~~~<>~<>

Hey, America's youth! I have some good news! In these muddled, mixed-up, mixed message-filled times we live in, there's still hope! And I mean 'youth' in a broad sense. Youth in general. Not you, over there sulking in the doorway, with your Goth eyeliner and all that impaled nose jewelry. But collectively speaking, there's still hope!

Yes, young people, you too can eventually sup on success, armed with nothing but your own initiative and ingenuity, a little luck, and millions in inherited trust funds strategically positioned in off-shore banks! You too can face universal loathing and be branded "The One Percent" by whining hippie wannabes whose idea of intensive career planning is to sleep in the park, dye their hair purple, and defecate on police cars!

(Okay, to be fair, that's not entirely true. They only dye *parts* of their hair purple.)

143

But I bring you today an assuring proof that the American Dream is still alive and kicking! And the best news is this - for you to dream the Dream, the same attainable, time-honored rules still apply:

- Stay in school, stay out of prison
- Build a website that caters to several hundred million insatiable egos and then sell it
- Floss

The proof? Facebook! The world's most popular hated website. Facebook - that ubiquitous online social platform that we all know and don't love.

Yesterday, in case you missed the financial news, facebook went public. This instantly made its creators, and Bono, very rich, and prompted the clever investment analysts at Morgan-Freeman-Stanley-Clark-Adam-Smith-Barney-Rubble   to immediately invest four billion dollars in MySpace.

The numbers are impressive, even to partly-purple people in tents. In just the first four minutes of its IPO, 100 million shares of facebook had been traded, mostly by Martha Stewart and members of the House Ethics Committee.

By the end of that first day, facebook's co-founder, Mark Zuckerberg, had some twenty billion dollars, prompting him to go buy a new wallet, and Brazil. As of right now, only twenty-eight people on Earth are richer than Zuckerberg, a guy who's younger than most of my shirts. Twenty billion bucks - not bad for someone who can't even drive after dark yet.

But what is it, exactly, that makes facebook so attractive to investors? To begin with, facebook is frugal; they didn't even spring for a capital F.

Furthermore, facebook has 800 million users, aka 'potential shoppers,' all connected to each other by various likes, dislikes, and other dysfunctional emotional states. Imagine that - 800 million captive consumers. If facebook were a country, it would be the fifth largest country on Earth, and Ron Paul would be demanding that we get our troops out of facebook.

And now that facebook has gone public, vested advertisers will have access to highly targeted markets; some seriously narrow niches: take, for example, your discriminating vampire. As it turns out, facebook vampires can be quite clique-ish. They're a lot like that famous golf club in Augusta GA where they hold the Masters, but with less plaid.

There are facebook groups for gay (or lesbian) vampires, Republican (or Democrat) vampires, vampire killers, vampire bikers, and, for all I know, suburban soccer mom vampires with fixed-rate mortgages who lease their Kia SUVs and take modest liberties on Schedule C deductions.

There are facebook groups for just about everything. And it's these groups, these connections between consumers that makes facebook so tempting to marketers. If someone with hundreds of facebook 'friends' buys something, they may share that news with all those friends. And those friends may share with *their* friends, and *those* may share, and on and on until the product goes viral, becomes all the rage, and no self-respecting metrosexual vampire would be caught undead without it.

And facebookers *will* share. Believe me, they'll share. They'll share that they decided to buy that thing, and what they were eating at the time, and how it tasted LOL, and what they plan to eat later BTW, and that now they're leaving to go buy that thing, they're on the way, they're almost there, and they almost drove past it cause they were updating their facebook status LOL. They'll share until you want to hit 'em with a golf club, or Ron Paul.

Facebook keeps track of how many 'friends' you have, a number which, for me, rises and falls as my friends rate my status updates, based on the following scale:

- Stupid
- More stupid
- Way more stupid
- Joe Biden

Today, for example, facebook tells me I have almost 800 friends.

No, I don't.

I don't have 800 friends. I don't even know 800 people. Heck, I don't know 800 *numbers*. In fact, by my count, I know exactly fourteen numbers:

- 0 through 9
- Less

- More
- Way more
- Theater popcorn

Of course, now that investors are involved, one has to wonder how much longer facebook will be free to use. And imagine having to handle billing for 800 million irate customers! Will there be some furiously underfunded office somewhere, similar to my cable company's Customer Service center? Some drab, concrete-block structure that's intentionally difficult to find, even harder to find parking, and staffed by two angry, obese women using circa 1979 black-and-white computer terminals that are still damp after being bought in bulk at an auction held by a defunct Pakistani call center after a tsunami?

It could get tricky. After all, facebook users are a special breed, even *before* you factor in fanged transsexuals, the Pit Bull Awareness Coalition (yes, there is), and the Appreciation Centre for Cats That Look Like Hitler. (yes, there is)

Case in point: somebody recently held a facebook poll, asking people if they installed their toilet paper rolls in "Over" or "Under" mode.

Within the first hour, 13,148 people had actually taken the time to vote. And in a world like that, there's only one thing left to say:

LOL.

147

Barry Parham

Toy Envy

You can take the caveman out of the cave, but...
<>~<>~~~~~~~~~~<>~<>~~~~~~~~~~<>~<>

One day at home, while I was hurrying to get from one room to another, and back before forgetting why I needed to go to the other room in the first place, a TV commercial caught my attention.

In the commercial, an easily excited Announcer Person raved on and on about a revolutionary new garden hose. And then he challenged me personally. And I have to admit - he was right.

True, I lead a very comfortable life. Yes, I have all that I need, and then some. Nevertheless, the disembodied voice was right.

I do not own a garden hose that can pull a truck.

But my friends might.

And that, as any marketer will tell you, is all it takes to sell products to guys. The technical term is "Toy Envy."

Women are different. Women need to be dazzled, or repeatedly bombarded with logic or emotion, or at least lured by some vague promise of losing weight, or gaining shoes.

Not guys. To sell stuff to guys, all you need is a healthy dose of Toy Envy; preferably, a dose delivered by some sultry-eyed life form who's almost wearing a bikini while washing a car and trying to eat a cheeseburger the size of the Chrysler Building.

Convince a guy that another guy has something the first guy hasn't got, and you're on your way to making a sale. Stir in a string bikini and a sesame-seed bun, and you'll be closing early.

Toy Envy explains why a guy on a business trip gets so excited when the car rental company upgrades him to a full-size model. To some guys, getting a free upgrade is a symbol of advanced masculinity, like being knighted, or suddenly inheriting a brewery.

And it's not the *guy's* fault. Toy Envy is the 'gatherer' part of that whole 'hunter-gatherer' thing you sometimes see discussed in documentaries narrated by Mr. Spock, just before you click back to the Bikini Food Network. A guy can no more avoid Toy Envy that he could avoid staring at something he just scratched off his scalp. You might as well ask a guy to not shake up a bottle of champagne.

Toy Envy is what lets a guy rationalize buying a $30,000 truck even though he can barely afford to keep gas in that '78 Dodge Dart with the duct-taped taillights. When challenged, Toy Envy will step up in front of the guy and say, "Well, you know, one day we might need to, like, haul something. You never know."

But there's a cost to society: Toy Envy is responsible for some of the dumbest commercials ever created. (One could create an entire documentary on this topic alone, if one cared enough, and one doesn't. Besides, Mr. Spock won't return one's calls.)

So let's just touch on two or three of the most absurd samples:

~-~-~-~-~-~

"WE'RE BROKE, BUT WE'RE LOOKIN' GOOD"

Maybe you've noticed. All these chiseled, successful guys that appear in our commercials have something you don't: cool clothes.

Okay, they're also taller, and sexier...and educated...and employed. True, they all have piercing steel-gray eyes and sculpted jaws that somehow always sport the perfect five-o-clock shadow. And their hair harbors more mousse than most Canadian national parks.

But times have changed. These days, a sense of style is way more important than sincerity or substance. These days, Shallow rules.

So right now, it's buy one, get one free, on most everything in the store. Because, let's face it - you're stuck with dull and ugly. But you can always drop a barge-load of money on more clothes.

And some mousse.

Because here at the Men's Easily-Bruised Ego Warehouse, you're gonna like the way you think you look.

And we're gonna like the way you look when you see your bill...I guarantee it.

~-~-~-~-~-~

"YOU CAN TRUST ME - I'M NOT TALENTED ENOUGH TO LIE"

Hi. I'm Murphy Slaw, an utterly forgettable former actor with white hair and fabulous polished teeth. You may remember me from my string of nearly memorable roles in a string of television mini-series, but I doubt it.

As you can see, I'm wearing a plaid flannel shirt and other borrowed clothes, and I'm standing next to a bunch of firewood while awkwardly wielding this absurdly heavy rube-maiming tool that I'm told is called an 'axe.'

And that's why I want you to invest in gold.

Like you, I worked hard for my money, if you define 'working hard' as getting flown around the world to spend 20 seconds regurgitating five memorized lines of dialogue. And based on that...and the axe...I'm apparently qualified to give you complex diversification-based financial advice.

So buy your gold where I buy mine. Because I don't have to tell you: times are tough, and getting tougher. In fact, while you're out, you might wanna pick up an axe.

~-~-~-~-~-~

"BECAUSE EVERY MAN SHOULD HAVE 250 SUITS"

This weekend only! at Joseph's A Bank! Buy one suit, get twenty-seven additional suits, absolutely free! Or buy any two shirts at our ridiculous regular price of $124.95 each, and get thirty-four shirts, 115 faux silk ties, and an unmatched tube sock, absolutely free!

That's right! This week only, at Joseph's A Bank, we got guys' casual sweaters made from rich Corinthian leather, six dozen for fourteen cents; we got men's lace-up terry-cloth turtleneck pajamas, priced to move at a nickel a gross; and don't forget - here at Joseph's A Bank, you'll find the East Coast's finest selection of neon aglets and cashmere dress shoes for that discerning carney on the go!

Craving retro? We got men's designer dickies, hand-made and tastefully dyed by caged, sullen Burmese primates trained to do simple knitting by eight manacled Irish barmaids who were captured during a bus tour and are now under the "care" of Kathie Lee Gifford.

How can we offer these insane prices, and these equally insane discounts? Easy - we just make stuff up. Prices, sales, specials, whatever. We just make up prices, call in the ads, and then go to lunch. Who knows; after lunch, we may jack the prices back up. One vest? Seven hundred dollars. Buy one dress shirt, get sixteen vests, absolutely free! Whee!

See, here at Joseph's A Bank, we don't care about profit. Why? Because the founder of Joseph's A Bank, Herod Joseph, doesn't care about profit. Herod Joseph owns about 4 kabillion investment firms in the Middle East, six Singapore sweat shops, and a federal credit union in Bethesda. I mean, the man's got more money than Joe Biden's dentist.

He's practically a walking ATM. That's right - here at Joseph's A Bank, Herod Joseph's a bank!

What? Oh. Yeah, I know, I know - *last* week, we warned you that our big sale was 'this week only.' And the week before that, too. Yeah, yeah, yeah.

But hey! Whaddaya want? Honesty? Or free stuff?

Yeah, that's what we thought.

The Stratocaster Effect

My, what a large Hadron you have!
<>~<>~~~~~~~~~<>~<>~~~~~~~~~<>~<>

Did you hear? They found God. He's in Switzerland.

That would explain the chocolate.

Actually, they only found a piece (God, not the chocolate). What they found was some subatomic thing scientists are calling the "god particle." And, based on all the high-fiving, toasting, and extremely lame dancing going on in scientist singles' bars, this discovery is the biggest thing since monogrammed lab goggles.

With the discovery of this *god particle*, the scientific world looks to have confirmed four things:

1) All matter was probably created by a subatomic scientist named Bo Higgs
2) All matter is probably held together by an analogy starring Justin Bieber
3) Probability Theory is probably 50% wrong, though they could be wrong

157

4)   Richard Dawkins just flat-out refuses to shampoo

But first, some background. We realize that not everybody speaks fluent scientist; besides, we're talking about the theoretical existence of particles so small that it would take six of them to make France surrender.

For years, physicists had been trying to explain the subatomic world using something known as the Standard Model, so named because physicists, as a rule, don't have very large Marketing budgets. However, the Standard Model had a gaping flaw, if we can use the word "gaping" to describe something smaller than Joe Biden's collection of Pink Floyd albums. But Physics was stuck with the Standard (see *Marketing budgets*), so they needed some way to fill that gap.

See, their model had no mechanism to explain why some particles seem to be massless (like the photon, which is not only the quantum bit for light, but also our primary defense against Klingons), while other particles have varying degrees of mass (W and Z bosons, practicing Catholics, Marlon Brando).

According to Physics, all particles should be without mass, zipping around freely and unrestrained, like Justin Bieber or Joe Biden.

For years, physicists were at a loss to explain this subatomic weight gain, this one-off oddity, and most universities didn't have the budget to spring for a hypothetical exception - what's known as a 'singularity' (literal translation: 'unmarried arity').

And then, along came the Higgs boson.

The Higgs boson was hypothesized in the 1960s by two Brits, Peter Higgs and Eric Clapton. Theoretically, its mechanism set up a field (named "Sally") that interacts with particles to endow them with mass, much like eating a meal prepared by Paula Dean. And the Higgs boson is the particle associated with that hypothetical field.

For over forty years, physicists had to simply assume that the Higgs field existed; meanwhile, there was overwhelming evidence to prove the existence of Eric Clapton. But in order to keep getting grant money from the Federal Stimulus Czars In Charge Of Stimulating Federal Stimulus Czars, the Physics departments had to either come up with a plausible explanation or start selling Buicks.

But because these theoretical particles were, well, theoretical, the desperate scientists had to settle for using analogies. And because I'm not good enough to make this stuff up, one of the analogies they came up with was...

Justin Bieber.

The analogy goes something like this: Imagine a cocktail party, but one that's cool, not one filled with socially awkward scientists arguing over disparate lime covalent ratios in theoretical Mai-Tais. Normal sane guests and celebrity stalker guests easily move back and forth across the room, unimpeded by the presence (mass) of the other guests, unless one of the other guests is a singularity, like film-maker Michael Moore, who has such a mass of mass that other, smaller film-makers are trapped in an orbit around him. (what astronomers call 'moons' and what we call 'sycophants')

But, continuing with our cocktail party analogy, when a celebrity like Justin Bieber shows up, all the wide-eyed fame-stricken guests press around him so tightly that he can hardly hit either of his two notes ... and then, once he and his hair begin to move, the crowd are bonded to him in such a way that the unified group become a nearly unstoppable force, like Al Sharpton when he sees a microphone.

And in case you're still buying any of this analogy bilge, here's the payoff: The crowd are massless particles, the celeb stalkers are Higgs bosons, and Justin Bieber is a massive Z boson.

And that, kids, is how everything in the universe was formed, except for Richard Dawkins.

Go ahead. Admit it. You just don't get hard science like this from most humor columns.

Moving from the theoretical to the practical, however, requires the physicists to adopt a different mindset. And most physicists I know are guys. And most guys I know equate "practical" with one of four things:

1) Women
2) Food
3) Women who brought food
4) Blowing stuff up

So naturally, some guys decided that the best way to get a Higgs boson to behave, to get it to come when you called it, was to blow it up.

What this particular particle challenge wanted was a super-powerful particle smasher, something that would produce energies violent enough to knock a Higgs boson into existence. And since the *Jerry Springer Show* was already booked, the scientists rang up Switzerland, known for countless generations as the go-to country when one wants unbridled violence, or hot chocolate.

Nestled in a non-disclosed location outside Geneva is one of humankind's crowning achievements: Brigitte Bardot. But in a tunnel nearby is the Large Hadron Collider (LHC), Earth's largest and highest-energy closed-loop accelerator, if you don't count NASCAR.

A collaboration by the European agency CERN, the LHC hopes to answer some of the most fundamental questions in Physics by deploying the time-honored tactic of full-contact violence. The LHC is a 17-mile concrete-lined ring, specifically designed to accelerate protons and then smash them into each other, the quantum equivalent of a *Three Stooges* sketch.

When the LHC is running at its full design power of 7 TeV per beam, protons will excite at discrete intervals until they have a Lorentz factor of 7,500 and move at about 0.999 999 991c in a superconducting dipole magnet field of 8.3 teslas, as you would expect, and you probably figured that out already, and you're lying.

The LHC gang had been slamming stuff into stuff for decades. They'd already defined the pro-Higgs scatter patterns that would match their theories. They'd already collected data for roughly a quadrillion proton-on-proton collisions. (they used really big legal pads) They'd been exciting protons at every opportunity, including some protons of questionable age.

And then, earlier this summer, all their efforts apparently paid off. Somewhere in that tesla-dripping tunnel, during one of those quad-whatever collisions, something ticked on somebody's monitor.

And suddenly it was Party Time, in a sad, pathetic, smart-people-who-don't-get-out-much kind of way.

Some threshold was achieved, some theoretical condition met. Some sensor chirped, some console lit up. A gauge red-lined, knocking a Brigitte Bardot calendar into an iPod's 'play' button. Wailing riffs from Eric Clapton's "Old Love" sparked through the tunnel.

Nobody moved, nobody dared breathe. Time stood still, although it can't. And then...there it was.

Peeking out from behind a bruised, dizzy proton - there it was. The universal constant. The grail. The glue that binds our whole universe.

The Higgs boson.

And standing behind the boson, representing the other proton in the collision ...

Celebrity attorney Gloria Allred.

Barry Parham

Welcome to the Zen's Wearhouse

You're gonna like the way you like you - I guarantee it
<>~<>~~~~~~~~~~<>~<>~~~~~~~~~~~<>~<>

Are you a tweep?

If there are any youngsters out there reading this, you should know that, not that long ago, asking a question like that could get you arrested, hit in the nose, or, depending on what State you lived in, engaged to someone with questionable teeth.

But now, as everybody knows, "tweep" is just a new addition to the American lexicon, a term that, roughly translated, means "the sound a bird makes when it's being censored."

I made that up. I do that, you know, from time to time. Sometimes I just make stuff up, in order to frustrate any publishers who might be toying with the idea of actually acknowledging one of my books, thereby making me rich and famous.

No, a tweep is a person who has an account at Twitter, that *other* wildly successful social media platform. (Twitter is sharing its success, of course, with facebook, that now-publicly traded company who's losing money so fast they can't even afford to buy a capital F.)

Now, there are some Twitter purists who'll say a tweep is a Twitter *message*, not a Twitter *user*. Yes, there really *are* such purists, and they have long, heated, unimaginably dull debates online, and if you know of anything more wretched than that, please share it with us. (tweet that tweep to @my_peeps #lemming)

I'm a tweep, along with some 150 million other people. And that's why I brought this up: not long ago, one of those 150 million other tweeps tweeted me, offering to be my 'life coach' and, as she put it, help me "get my Zen on!"

Really. That's really what she said. Get my Zen on.

Get my Zen on? Yikes. That may be the ugliest cultural collision I've personally witnessed since that awful day when John Denver started covering Bob Marley tunes.

Get my Zen on. Whoa. Girlfriend's, like, down in six with my koan and stuff, and awareness is in the house, home tweepies. Satori, fuh shizzle. (To be honest, I'm not entirely sure what I just said there, so if I insulted you, please forgive me and blame George Bush.)

My very own life coach. Because I have the utmost respect for all these "Let me help you with your self-help" entrepreneurs, I'll call her Aura Babe. In her tweep and at her website, Aura Babe wants you to know that she is an Internationally Certified Visual Coach. (I don't know where she got her International

Certification, but I'm guessing Photoshop was involved.) Aura Babe assures me that there are only a very few ICVCs in the whole world, and I would go beyond calling that a mere fact - I would call that a blessing. (I don't know how the relevant authorities manage the globally available pool of Visual coaches, but I'm guessing a statute of limitations is involved.)

And *what*, as you probably would never think to ask if you lived to be 130, is Visual Coaching anyway? Well, 'visual coaching' is an acquired skill that, according to Aura Babe, involves coaching visually (I'm not good enough to make this stuff up). In fact, Aura Babe has even coined a phrase for her technique: Meditation and Manifestation with Markers.

As her website states, by using the time-honored M&M/M techniques, you will learn to focus your attention - for brief periods of time - just by doodling with colored markers! Isn't that amazing? Aura Babe really puts the "magic" in "magic marker," eh?

(You and I, at one point in our lives, would've called this "coloring." And afterwards, we would each be handed half a graham cracker, and then - Nap Time.)

The site's FAQ page explains that "Image coaching" lets you discover "images" that "speak" to you so you can tell your "story." We would like the FAQ page to know that all that cute "use" of quotes is very "irritating."

See, Aura Babe knows that 86% of us learn visually. Or maybe she doesn't know; on another page, she says 65% of us learn visually. (I wonder if Aura Babe knows that 100% of us *proofread* 100% visually, although proofing won't "stop" anybody from making up "goofy" phrases like "get your Zen on.")

But when one chooses to surrender oneself to the ministrations of an Internationally Certified Visual Coach, why, successfully donning one's Zen is just the beginning.

Once you're in the capable hands of Aura Babe:

- You can unleash your moxie.
- You can stand in your sacred self's tallness.
- You can experience deep connection without having to care for anyone else (exactly what you're connecting to, I don't even want to guess)
- You can up-level your mindset.
- You can quiet your Inner Critic, not to mention your Itty Bitty Doubting Committee.
- Instead of cowing to the Bitty Committee, you can tune in to your Inner Whisper.
- You can become an active co-creator of your own life (I'm not sure how that works, but don't listen to me - most of my Zen's still at the dry cleaners).
- You can brainstorm ways to monetize your passion. (This ... again, depending on your jurisdiction ... is called prostitution.)

And don't think for a minute that you're not capable of being all you can be. Splattered across the website are motivational soul-warmers like this: You got moxie up the wazoo!

On the other hand, there's this online warning:

IMPORTANT: This Retreat is NOT for everyone! If you are opposed to the law of attraction, healing energies, and other "woo-woo" concepts, this probably won't be a fit for you!

Woo-woo concepts. Because sometimes, a single woo concept is just not enough.

The cost? Bah! Here at the Co-Creator Fun Park and Crayon Self-Expression Sanctuary, there are no costs; there are only investments. The introductory session is a paltry $99, or $75, depending on the page you visit. So hang on - if this lady keeps building web pages, soon this whole weekend'll be free.

But no worries! If things just don't work out for you and your moxie's woo-woo, Aura Babe says refunds are "easy peasy!"

Hmm. I don't know about you, but I'm just not comfortable putting my tall moxie in the co-self-creating hands of some toothy peasant-skirted bimbo whose financial strategies include marginal mathematics like "easy peasy."

The Visual Coaching sessions are usually done in "one-one-one" settings, which either means Aura Babe is too busy being intuitive and non-Itty Bitty to bother with proofreading, or it means there'll be something going on that involves three people, and I personally don't care to be quite that intuitive.

Aura Babe coaches professional coaches, too, and promises to teach them the ability to earn more while doing less. This, she says, is a spiritual law of success. Coincidentally, it is also a good working definition of "civil service."

And speaking of slipshod work and no accountability whatsoever, Aura Babe points out that she loves to "do in person workshops!" So if you're a person workshop, you better sleep with one eye open! Somewhere out there is a woo-woo moxie uplifter looking to do you in.

And finally...

Note to Aura Babe: Your web pages have several "Page Not Found" problems, so check your website's links, and do it often. It's not easy peasy, but abandoning a person's pre-uplifted moxie in a dark, navigational dead end is not conducive to visually monetizing one's wazoo.

Fuh shizzle.

And For Afters?

~*~*~

"Life is uncertain. Eat dessert first."

Ernestine Ulmer

~   *~*

"When dining with a demon, you got to have a long spoon."

Navjot Singh Sidhu

~*~*~*~

Après-calypse

What if you threw an armageddon and nobody came?
<>~<>~~~~~~~~~~<>~<>~~~~~~~~~~<>~<>

*"Twas the night before nothing, and all through the Vedic Seventh House,
Not a creature was stirring, not even a Tzotzil-Tzeltal Hun-Ahpu."*

So, fellow Earthlings - we made it! 21 December 2012 is now behind us, and we're still here! No global disaster. No earthquake or tidal wave, no volcanic eruption, no communications disruption. No meteor strike, no meteorological stroke, no fireball rainstorm. No societal collapse, except Detroit. No invading aliens or scary monsters, unless you count John Kerry and his Giant Pointy Chin of Death.

After all the hubbub, here we are...the Saturday everybody was betting against. Day One of the Fourteenth Mayan Baktun (literal translation: *"kosher bakery"*). The most wager-loaded weekend in the history of mankind, outside of All-Saints Bingo Night at the Vatican, and Chicago politics.

My, my. Has another baktun really come and gone? Seems like only yesterday, we were ushering in a fresh new Thirteenth

Baktun (literal translation: *"baker's dozen"*) with a hearty 'Toxlpretnik.' (literal translation: *"Yo! Nice pretnik!"*)

But as cataclysmic galaxy-disrupting end-of-all-things events go, this one was a real naval-gazer. I've seen more carnage at the grocery on "Expired Milk Day." This latest Mayan death-to-all-fest was about as yawny as Hillary Clinton, deflecting a Congressional hearing or a conjugal offer ("Not tonight, dear. I have a *ferocious* diplomatic immunity.")

No, this apoca-lapse will doubtless be ranked on the excite-o-meter somewhere between a black-and-white rerun of "An Andy Williams Labor Day Singalong" and Michael Moore's five-hour-long, critically-panned documentary, "REM Sleep," starring Lindsay Lohan as Nick Nolte.

Even the final curtain's schedule was clumsy and indecisive. Some doom-watchers determined that the world would end just after midnight Thursday; other fate-junkies had called it for dawn Friday (probably the people who have to clean the universe's bathrooms before the workday begins); still other eschatology-hounds thought it would all be over, cosmically-speaking, at midnight Friday, as if the universe ran on the same principles as an off-campus beer bar. And Mexico's National Institute of Anthropology, History, and Colorful Beach Towels maintained that we'd all miscalculated the Mayan Long Count anyway, and so the *real* last Last Call would actually take place sometime the following Sunday.

(It's contrarian nonsense like that, of course, that helps explain why nobody's ever heard of Mexico's National Institute of Anthropology, History, and Colorful Beach Towels.)

But it was a false alarm, as everyone now knows (except for CNN, who are still calling it an apocalyptic "trend"). And hindsight, as they say, is 20-20, especially if you're having hindsight *and* your planet wasn't vaporized.

Leading up to the non-event event, however, Earthlings everywhere were gearing up for something big. It was like a global conference of people who talk to invisible rabbits named Harvey, if all those people also wore robes, dream-catcher earrings, Birkenstocks, and were all named Zed the Scar, or Endive.

On that non-fateful Friday, 21 December 2012, if any particular place on Earth could've been called "downtown Doomsday," that place would be Merida, in the Mexican Yucatan, home to the Mayan complex known as Chichen Itza. (literal translation: *"Chicken Little."* See? See how it's all starting to come together?)

In ancient Mayan culture, Chichen Itza was a sort of Roman Coliseum, according to a recently unearthed 5,000-year-old episode of that Mesoamerican hit game show, "Who Wants to Eat the Internal Organs of a Millionaire?" And on Faux Friday, there were more free spirits at Chichen Itza than there are pot-smokers at a Detroit auto plant.

But apparently, based on the reported clouds of pot and patchouli at Chichen Itza's Armless-geddon, America's auto unions were well-represented. Reporters noted an abundance of joint-huffers among the tree-huggers. In fact, there at

Chicken Little Central during D-Day, it was a sort of bohemian Noah's Ark.

There were Buddhists, druids, pagans, Republicans, and one guy wearing a seriously un-subtle skull ornament that was either a large, caffeine-crazed bird or an Elton John costume. Situated around ceremonial fires at the pyramid known as El Castillo, robed moon-eyed people chanted and blew into conch shells, perhaps in simulated worship of some primeval breathalyzer.

"We are in a new vibration," proclaimed self-proclaimed spiritual master, Ollin Yolotzin, who won the event's award for "Coolest Spiritual Master Name" and is also the head of an Aztec dance group Cuautli-balam (literal translation: *"Glee"*).

"We are in a frequency of love," gasped the master, as he blew on a conch. Sadly, though, the frequency wore off fairly quickly - Vibration Boy nearly got arrested for conch-honking without a valid Apocalypse permit.

And then there was Gabriel, a Los Angeles-based spiritualist who claimed to embrace no "silly theatrics" about Friday's no-pocalypse, while unpacking his ceremonial crystal skulls. He said this with a straight face.

Also in attendance at the Unarmored-geddon was one Dr. Nina, a minor celebrity among the baby doomers at Chicken Little, who pointed to her with their damp conchs and said she was "possibly the best credentialed spiritualist in attendance." (literal translation: *"Yo! Nice tin-foil hat!"*)

You Gonna Finish That Dragon?

Dr. Nina is president of a panel devoted to "pioneering consciousness" and another group that's dedicated to "conscious evolution," so she is obviously the go-to lady when you need some quick consciousness, or when you've overdone it on the patchouli. Dr. Nina is also known as one of the "Notable Luminaries of Evolutionary Leaders," and I got five bucks that says there's no such group. (If there *is* such a group, I'm guessing they gave *themselves* the twenty-five-dollar name "Notable Luminaries" at an emergency meeting of the Self-Aggrandizement Olympics.)

"I'm here to recommit myself to being free of attachments," said Doc Nina, as she huddled to meditate in front of a small Mayan temple decorated with jaguar heads. ·

No worries, Doc. What with your going on and on about all that luminous pioneer jaguar consciousness, I'm guessing that you'll be free of attachments for several weekends. No worries at all.

Of course, even though the Chick-fil-A Pyramids were getting the Mayan's share of attention on Final Friday, there were Doom-Watches going on all over Earth. In England, a man calling himself Arthur Uther Pendragon showed up at Stonehenge and whipped the Druids into a short-lived frenzy, at least until the Druids learned that Arthur Uther's real name was John Timothy Rothwell; once the Druids found *that* out, they beat him unconscious with a "Monty Python & the Holy Grail" DVD.

In central China, a group claimed that Jesus had reappeared as a woman (fortunately, there were no "Monty Python's Life of

Brian" side-effects). In Detroit public schools, classes were canceled, making it difficult for anyone to buy guns and drugs. In France, a group gathered in the Pyrenees to surrender to a spaceship, or anything else that showed up.

In San Diego, a man was detained by police just for wearing a gas mask and a machete. I mean, c'mon ... in Southern California, that's just work-a-day attire for the morning commute. For UPS drivers in Detroit, it's standard issue.

But in our opinion, the best Apocalypse (Just Not) Now anecdote of all comes from Bolivia, that little landlocked central South American country whose primary exports are tin, cocaine, and Bolivians.

According to local reports, Bolivian President Evo Morales was ferried, on a wooden raft, to a small island in the middle of Lake Titicaca (literal translation: *"Yo! Nice Tetons!"*), where festive tin-snorting locals made sacrificial offerings to Pachamama (Mother Earth), Machu Picchu Mama (Middle-Aged Cougar Lady), and Nacho Mama. (you do realize I'm making up these names, right?)

Meanwhile, back at Chicken Little: we met "Angela," who flew down from Seattle to finally meet the aliens who originally brought human DNA to Earth - and, based on recent human behavior, the DNA delivery wasn't all that long ago. Obviously overwhelmed by her surroundings, Angela waxed poetic while contemplating the mind-boggling, mist-shrouded El Castillo pyramid looming behind her: she called it "an edgy tower."

She said "edgy tower." Seriously.

Back home in the Pacific Northwest, Angela teaches driver's ed.

Seriously.

By the way: Angela's friend and traveling companion, "Sarah," thinks that our alien-sourced DNA might once have granted us the ability to do amazing things: to see underwater, or to fly, or to like totally eat donuts without getting like way fat and stuff.

"I'm not sure, though," Sarah warns. "These are theories."

Seriously.

Barry Parham

The Search for Intelligent Life...and Pizza

Does my calling plan cover Betelgeuse, or is that 'roaming?'
<>~<>~~~~~~~~~<>~<>~~~~~~~~~~<>~<>

It's official.

Thanks to NASA, we now have the proof: Tom Cruise is *not* the smallest life form in the universe.

Earlier this year, astronomers announced the discovery of the smallest planet in the known universe, a planet so tiny that it could support Gerard Depardieu, or Joy Behar, but not both. Planet Kepler-37B, named after the Kepler Space Telescope, proves two things about NASA: they remain relevant in difficult financial times, and they have no budget money left for the Department In Charge of Naming New Planets.

Pint-sized planet Kepler-37B (let's call her "Keppie") was spotted in the constellation Lyra, and is the third planet we've discovered in the Lyra sector. Upon hearing about Lyra having all these planets running around getting discovered all over the place, two disgruntled neighboring constellations (Drachma and Guilder) sued the universe for unfair distribution of tiny planetoids, and emotional cruelty. The litigating star systems are being represented by celestial celebrity attorney, Gloria Allred.

Relatively speaking, Keppie is right next door - just 210 light-years away from Earth. 'Light-year' is a technical term used by astronomers (an 'Astronomer' is someone who makes a living studying the Jetson's dog).

It's a complicated concept, the light-year, but in layman's terms the principle works something like this: if an astronomer was given 12 months' worth of free beer, a light-year represents the amount of time the astronomer would spend excusing himself to go to the "Little Astronomer's room."

('Light-year' is one of several suave ice-breakers that astronomers use to pick up chicks in bars, which explains the high incidence of unmarried astronomers.)

(In a related story, my referring to women as 'chicks' probably helps explain my steady record of non-nuptial-ness.)

Now, to the average Earthling, the discovery of yet another space rock is hardly exciting news; it's not like it was another NASCAR mangling, or a Kardashian sighting. However, to the science community, this find was right up there with water on Mars, or taco shells made out of Doritos. In fact, one of the world's most famous planet-hunters, Duane 'Dog-Star' Chapman, put it this way: "Once again, guys who study the Jetson's dog are able to offer proof that the universe contains an incredibly diverse parade of planets: planets of all shapes and sizes, as long as you define 'shapes' as 'round.'"

Kepler-37B was actually discovered over a year ago, by a government employee in California who was killing time while waiting for his taxpayer-funded sex change operation. And then other scientists got involved (with the new planet, not the sex change). And then it happened: somebody called a meeting.

And a year passed.

It was awful. Endless. Meetings, everywhere, every day. Is Keppie a planet? Or just a moon? Is it a *small* planet, or a *dwarf* planet? Is it habitable and conducive to civilization, or more like Detroit?

And on it went. Over-caffeinated, under-funded lab assistants, arguing with under-qualified, overpaid government experts. There were flip charts; pie charts; pivot charts; PowerPoints. There were hordes of gophers, steadily caravanning tankards of soured coffee and tepid slices of carry-out pizza. There were 247 failed attempts to successfully initiate a conference call.

Finally, though it took nearly a year, science reached a verdict, and now we have a new planet. Immediately, Verizon dispatched a sales fleet to convince the planet's teenagers to switch cell phone providers.

Sadly for Verizon stockholders, though, astronomers concede that the diminutive planet is not likely to support life; after all, the surface temperature is around 700 degrees Fahrenheit, about the same as Phoenix in March. On the other hand, with that kind of pre-heated planet, the tiny citizens of Kepler-37B could whip up a really fast carry-out pizza.

"Thanks for calling Parsec Pizza, once again voted the least tepid carry-out this side of the Neutral Zone! Delivery in under thirty light-years, guaranteed, or it's free! Don't forget to ask about our weekly special: a ten Galactic Credit discount for new Verizon customers!"

Over the light-years, astronomers claim to have made many contributions to science, and I bet there are some. For example, if it weren't for astronomy, we might never know to snort condescendingly in movie theaters when spaceships blow up and make loud *'BLAM'* noises. I mean, c'mon. Everybody knows that in the still, empty vacuum of outer space, exploding spaceships can't make a loud *'BLAM'* noise. (They make a loud *'KABOOM'* noise.)

So how did these astronomers find little Keppie, anyway? Well, just like any other group of guys who can't get a date, astronomers have their own little bag of tricks. One of their planet detection schemes works like this: the goal is "to spot the wobble that a star's spectrum would display from the gravitational tug of an orbiting planet."

Now try and tell me *that* pickup line wouldn't bring a caring woman to tears.

In the past, a search technique was sometimes employed that examined a target area for brightness, but that plan was abandoned after somebody aimed the brightness-o-meter at a network TV executive. The poor device got such a null reading that it committed suicide.

(Alternatively, astronomers will sometimes use a detection strategy that has something to do with monitoring sound waves moving through hot gas, and in our opinion, the less said about that, the better.)

Then, once they *have* found a planet, even a very small one, the next step is determining if there's life there, even if the life forms are so small, even Gloria Allred won't return their calls.

According to that raucous literary crowd-pleaser, an annual publication named the *Astronomers Light-Yearly*, what five things make a planet potentially livable?

1) Oxygen (the gas, not the TV channel)
2) An energy source (unless it's North Korea, or BP)
3) Carbon (so the environmentalists will have something to whine about)
4) Silicon (don't mind that noise - it's just the single astronomers, giggling)
5) Carry-out pizza

Speaking of years, Kepler-37B is so tiny, and so close to its own sun, that its whole year only lasts 13.4 Earth days - less than two weeks! Imagine such a planet. Even worse, imagine the single astronomers' lame jokes:

Their year's so short...

- they don't have annual physicals - they just mail the doctor a check, then go off and die
- the top news magazine is a CBS show named *Two-and-a-Quarter Minutes*
- AARP starts bombarding them with endless, insistent membership mailings when they're barely 18 months old

By the way, here are some "just how small *was* that life form?" knee-slappers that are popular among astronomers in singles bars:

- "That life form was so small, a quark took his lunch money."
- "That life form is so small, they look up to Dennis Kucinich. Literally."
- "That life form was so small, his carry-on baggage checked *him*."

Sad, isn't it.

So here's to you, Team NASA and the Kepler sky-eye. Well done! Planet discovered; mission accomplished; bill paid. And all of us down here wish you well as you embark on your next mission:

The search for intelligent life in Congress.

Actually, I made that up. *Nobody's* got that kind of time. Not even NASA.

My Short Stint at Hallmark

Would Cupid's bow be a sexual assault weapon?
<>~<>~~~~~~~~~~<>~<>~~~~~~~~~~<>~<>

Valentine's Day, once again, has come and gone. And in cozy dens all across America, guys are staring bitterly at oversized, under-performing teddy bears.

Guys have learned to accept the rule: *you never forget Valentine's Day.* We understand that Valentine's Day is a beast that must be fed. And in the middle of February, it's not like we have a lot of options. The Super Bowl's over. It's either this little spending jag, or watch league bowling.

According to the internet, Valentine's Day shoppers will spend around $17 billion this year, which is about what Congress spends each week on coffee creamer, or Altoids. (with an eleventh-hour amendment to grant funding, in an up-for-grabs voting district in Colorado, for research into reggae music's effects on the stress levels of popcorn shrimp at high altitudes)

For Valentine's Day, the average guy will spend about $170, which means that most of the guys I know are *way* below average.

(By the way, the average woman will spend about half that much. Unless she's in Congress.)

Interesting to note: when it comes to forking it out for Valentine's Day, the top spending city in America is that odd oven of a place where the temperature regularly hits 195 degrees but the residents will still say, with a straight face, "Yeah, but it's a dry heat." The #1 city in V-Day spending? Phoenix, Arizona.

But it's a dry spending.

And in the highly profitable greeting card industry, no holiday can touch Valentine's Day. (Well, there's that one holiday in December, that messy, controversial one we've been celebrating for 2,000 years but can't anymore because it offends four petulant people. But we'll probably ban that one soon, anyway, so...)

Some 150 million variously-Valentine-tainted cards will be purchased and delivered; most of them, thanks to that "Forever" stamp farce, with insufficient postage.

But while trolling the V-Day section in the greeting card aisle, I notice a need for some niche marketing. Some specialization. Every year, the same old suitors, sharing the same old sentiments with the same old, uh, suitees.

And, as always, I'm here to help. In case Hallmark needs some fresh ideas, here are some romantic verses.

You Gonna Finish That Dragon?

Well, here are some verses, anyway.

~-~-~-~-~-~

From: the Rookie

~-~-~

Roses are red
Violets are blue
Sure, I'll co-sign your car loan!
Pay your VISA bill, too!

~-~-~-~-~-~

From: the Tightwad

~-~-~

Roses are red
And they cost too much, too
But this candy's on sale
So I bought some for you

~-~-~-~-~-~

From: the Neurotic

~-~-~

Roses are red
Or that's what they say
At my therapy session
Every other Wednesday

~-~-~-~-~-~ .

From: the Princess

~-~-~

For roses, I flutter
For diamonds, I simmer

But what I deserve
Is a spanking new Bimmer

~-~-~-~-~-~

From: Ohio voters
To: Barack Obama

~-~-~

How do I love thee?
Let me miscount the ways.

~-~-~-~-~-~

From: Mayor Bloomberg
To: New York City

~-~-~

Guns are forbidden
Salt is taboo
If your soda's too hefty
The city will sue

~-~-~-~-~-~

From: the Slimeball

~-~-~

Roses are red
Got my old lady a dozen
But I slipped up and mailed 'em
To Mona, her cousin

~-~-~-~-~-~

From: MSNBC
To: reporting staff

~-~-~

Roses are red

Violets are blue
Obama made the flowers
And kitty cats, too

~-~-~-~-~-~

From: Distracted

~-~-~

Roses are red
Whaddayacallit's are blue
The, uh...the thing I wante...um
Did I mention the roses?

~-~-~-~-~-~

From: Jilted

~-~-~

Roses are red.
Die in the street, witch.

~-~-~-~-~-~

From: Bill Clinton
To: Match.com

~-~-~

I used to be President
They all called me 'Slick'
I play a mean sax, and wa...
Hey, who's the chick?

~-~-~-~-~-~

From: Chicago voters
To: Barack Obama

~-~-~

We got votes from Club Med

191

We got votes from Peru
Heck, half our voters are dead
And they still vote for you
~-~-~-~-~-~-~

From: Agent Starling
To: Hannibal Lecter
~-~-~

The roses are nice
And thanks for the bunch
But I should've known better
When you said, "Let's do lunch."
~-~-~-~-~-~-~

From: Barack Obama
To: MSNBC
~-~-~

Some states are red
Good states are blue
You love me madly
And I love me, too
~-~-~-~-~-~-~

From: The First Michelle
To: America
~-~-~

Roses are red
Gimme some
~-~-~-~-~-~-~

From: Cynical
~-~-~

These "There's only you" cards
Won't fool many chicks
I notice they're bundled
In packets of six

~-~-~-~-~-~

From: Carnival Cruise Lines
To: 3,143 stranded passengers

~-~-~

Dark, heat, and dread
No food, lights, or view
Sorry about the head;
Here's a voucher for you!

~-~-~-~-~-~

From: White House Fund-Raising Committee
To: the CEO of Carnival Cruise Lines

~-~-~

Your diversion was perfect
With that "fire" from your crew
Thanks for the solid
Now here's *your* "voucher," too!

~-~-~-~-~-~

From: Gullible

~-~-~

Roses are red
Violets are blue
Though you're dating the Packers
I will always love you

~-~-~-~-~-~

From: Texting

~-~-~

fyi roses r red
+ voiltes r blue
omg I heart u 2 imho
lol

~-~-~-~-~-~

From: Barack Obama
To: Congress

~-~-~

So long, my darlings
Our love affair's through
I am so gonna run things
Without any of you

~-~-~-~-~-~

From: the Single Guy

~-~-~

Roses, they're buying
And teddy bears, too
I think I'll order another pizza and watch the game in socks
and a Nordic helmet
And nobody's all up in my face barking at me for slipping into
non-rhyming prose, either

~-~-~-~-~-~

From: Philadelphia voters
To: Barack Obama

~-~-~

How do I vote for thee?
Let me count the ways.

You Gonna Finish That Dragon?

~-~-~-~-~-~-~

From: Hillary Clinton
To: the US Senate

~-~-~-~

"I'm too busy," I said
Then came down with the flu
Next, I fell on my head
What difference does it make?

~-~-~-~-~-~-~

From: Press Secretary Jay Carney
To: the White House Press Corps (except FoxNews)

~-~-~-~

Roses are blue
Roses are red
Roses are blue
As the President has always said

~-~-~-~-~-~-~

From: Pope Benedict XVI
To: populum meum

~-~-~-~

Rosas sunt rubri
Violas caeruleae sunt
I'm still Pope for a while yet
So I'm not going anywhere *near* that rhyme

~-~-~-~-~-~-~

From: Joe Biden
To: any open microphone

~-~-~-~

Roses are crimson
Violets are teal
Valentine's Day
Is a big &*@$^#% deal

~-~-~-~-~-~-~

All that romance. All that emotion. All those stamps. Why, it makes my eyes moist.

But it's a dry moist.

So, Your Honor, By the Twelfth Day of Christmas

Where do you go to return twelve pear trees?
<>~<>~~~~~~~~~~<>~<>~~~~~~~~~~<>~<>

I don't know about you, but I'd pay real money to just skip the whole week after Christmas. There are several reasons why:

- Your waistline's fatter, but your wallet's thinner
- You have to go to work, but everybody else is on vacation, so it's impossible to get an approval, a signature, or sexually harassed
- Everybody at every store is returning stuff, including gifts, but also things like live animals, dead laptops, unwrapped undergarments, and suspect cheese
- You're stuck with sports options like the San Diego County Credit Union Poinsettia Bowl, the Franklin American Mortgage Music City Bowl, and the PETA Simpering Confiscatory Fund To Help Relocate The Transgendered Spackle-Necked Ozark Boll Weevil Bowl
- You still have seventeen rolls of cartoon-reindeer-coated gift-wrapping paper that can't possibly be used

for mid-calendar occasions like birthdays, weddings, and early parole celebrations

Plus, thanks to a Christmas-carol-induced purchasing frenzy, committed by My True Love (I call her "True"), I'm now several layers deep in redundant gifts ... 364 of 'em, if you add up all twelve days' worth.

The unmentioned problem with the whole *'Twelve Days of Christmas'* gift strategy is its multiplier effect. I mean, thanks very much, True, but ... twenty-two turtle doves? Seriously?

Maybe, I could find a use for *one* golden ring. *Maybe.* Ever unwrapped five of them? And then five more, and then five more? Eight times? While you're trying not to trip over maids, lords, pipers, drummers, geese, hens, swans, doves, calling birds and cranky PETA protestors?

And if you've ever had thirty heavily-caffeinated lords leaping in the same room with forty-two egg-laying geese, you know things aren't going to end well. That's just goose doom waiting to happen. That's just pending pâté.

Another problem with the week after Christmas is a sneaky post-Christmas music conspiracy. Here's how it works: During the holiday season, we're persistently bathed in happy, inspiring Christmas music, and it's wonderful. But then, once Christmas is over, the music gatekeepers box up the good stuff until next year.

And then they pull out the B team. Really marginal stuff. The fringe fa-la-la. Dick Haymes. Patti Page. Tex Ritter (I'm not kidding). Various amalgams called The So-And-So Brothers or The Whatsit Sisters, babbling about bells, fat men, fat men with coal, Mommy *kissing* fat men, and Frosty the Scary Reanimated Popsicle Person. Paul Anka from his "pre-acne" period (apparently Paul Anka has never been spotted *not* singing, and has at least two albums recorded *in utero*). The Ray Conniff Singers, who deserve to be publicly caned simply for horribly arranged syncopation. Roger Whittaker singing Boston Marathon versions of '*The Twelve Days,*' which may constitute criminal negligence and be legally actionable.

It's as if we'd all spent the last few months in a warm, cozy bar relishing the house band, led by Mozart himself, and suddenly we're stuck with a bad eight-track tape titled "Salieri Is Rocking This Crimmuh, Yo."

Case in point: not long ago, because I wasn't fast enough to turn off the radio, I heard somebody named Buddy Clark singing something called '*The Merry Christmas Waltz.*'

I'm still getting over it.

'*The Merry Christmas Waltz*' is, without challenge, the WASP-est holiday offering ever over-wrought. Compared to this arrangement, Lawrence Welk was the thug gangsta love child of Jimi Hendrix and Sergio Mendes.

"Wunnerful, wunnerful! Give it up one moe 'gin for Paul Anka's fetus and the June Taylor Dancers!"

Besides, there's something sinister about 3/4 time. It's just so ... feudal.

I understand what the gatekeepers are trying to do - they're trying to make us so sick of carols that we won't miss them when they go away until next winter. I understand. They're weaning us. They're trying to do us a favor.

Stop trying to do us a favor.

Conspiracies aside, though, America's Christmas music repertoire in general is out of control. Over time the genre has crab-walked into topics that are, at best, a bit of a stretch and, at worst, downright bizarre. Let's review some selected lyrics, shall we?

"Hang your nose down, Rudy. Hang your nose and cry."
What the heck is *that?*

"Here comes the fattest man in town."
C'mon, people. It's Christmas. Leave Newt alone.

"He's a rootin' tootin' Santa Claus. Yippee ki-yo ki-yay!"
This marketing tie-in defies analysis, and the absurdity speaks for itself. Besides, I don't want to know anyone who is rootin', much less tootin'.
And just for the record - if anybody ever walks up to me and says "yippee ki-yo ki-yay," I'll stab 'em with a pointy stick. If they're wearing a red wool suit, I'll stab twice.

"To see a great big man entirely made of snow," she sings.
This is an obvious, desperate plea for therapy. When the snow melts, somebody riffle the Yellow Pages for "intervention."

"Down in Mexico, we have got no snow. Every time we sing, tequila glasses ring."
Let's hope they don't sing much, else it's gonna be an early night. Have an undocumented Christmas!

"If you want bananas, great big bananas, shake hands with Santa Claus."
How does that transaction work, exactly? What, is St. Nick now moonlighting as some kind of Chiquita Pez dispenser? It sounds more like some sick Vegas come-on, or street code for a drug drop.

"Tumpety tum tum."
"Ba rum pa tum tum."
"Jing jing-a-ling ling-a-ling ling-a-ling-ling. Ha ha. Ho ho."
What more is there to say, your honor? Psychiatric evaluation completed. Case closed. Bring on the big-arm tuxedo.

Then there are songs that snuck in, like emaciated blonde celebrity addicts at a White House dinner, and now they won't go away. In our opinion, '*My Favorite Things*' is not a legitimate Christmas carol; however, it *is* a nice "hint hint, honey!" paean to obsessive shopping. And given everything American advertising has done to prostitute Christmas, the jury's still out on this one.

Nor is '*Toyland*' a valid tune for tinsel-time. "Once you cross its border, you can never return again" does *not* invoke Christmas. This is more a tune for Halloween, maybe, or a cautionary tale about backpacking in Iran's back yard. It speaks of making a bad decision with no mulligans, like subscribing to that relentless, time-defying Time-Life Book-of-the-Month club, or eating too much Mexican food.

And speaking of Halloween, what's the back story on this campfire lyric, from '*It's the Most Wonderful Time of the Year*' - "There'll be scary ghost stories and tales of the glories of Christmases long, long ago."

What glories, exactly? Dude, we're talking about a federal holiday, not the fields of Verdun or the '36 Olympics! Did I miss something on the news wire? Did Santa paratroop into Tehran and spirit away the busted backpackers?

But even those tunes, bad as they are, are mere infractions. As Gandalf might put it, there are fouler things in the deep places than Orcs. Musical travesties exist that must be stopped, with due prejudicial intensity and by all available means, military, judicial and otherwise. So, in the interest of promoting a sane, civil society, I propose a new set of Yuletide Music Management laws.

- In the song '*Jingle Bells*,' after the line "...O'er the hills we go, laughing all the way," it shall be illegal for a recording studio to insert actual laughter. This prohibition shall include (but not be limited to) the ha-ha-ha's of children, dogs, and strolling hordes of Lawrence Welk-type Judeo-Christian couples.
- No entity shall be allowed to add lyrics to Tchaikovsky's '*Nutcracker Suite*.'
- It doesn't make any sense for all-growed-up adults to be singing '*All I want for Christmas is my two front teeth*,' unless said adult is hopelessly accident-prone, or Leon

Spinks. So cease and desist. Find a kid or sit down. Estop it.

- During any given Christmas tune, you may only transpose up to the next key once. Actually, the court would prefer that you not transpose at all or, if possible, less.

- It shall be illegal for anyone, anywhere, at any time, to sing '*Dominick, the Christmas Donkey.*' Not even as a joke. This proscription really should've been part of the original U.S. Constitution.

- The Rule of Thirds: If a carol is written in a perfectly nice minor key and then suddenly, at the very end of the song, you decide to resolve it in a major key, the court will find you and visit upon you a severe form of vigilante justice. (see "pointy stick")

- No one shall be allowed to modify, in any way, '*The Twelve Days of Christmas.*' This carol is much like the Constitution - it may have its flaws, but futzing around with it is only gonna make things worse.

In closing, I'll confess something to you. As much as I love the holiday season, there's one American-holiday-oriented thing I'm always glad to know will be going away - wherever it is these things go away to - until next Christmas. And what is that thing, you ask?

Burl Ives.

It's nothing personal, actually, even though there's something about Burl's cover of '*Frosty the Snowman*' that makes True and me want to invest in an ice axe. No, my main concern is this: I just want to make darn sure the gatekeepers have big Burl available, until next holiday season, to sit on the box where they keep Andy Williams.

You know what I'm saying? I mean, the average American's work-a-day year is hard enough already.

The *last* thing we need in mid-calendar is Andy Williams jumping up and grinning those teeth at us.

Olympic Segue XXX

And so it ends, except it never ends

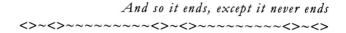

If you heard a huge crash this week, don't worry about it. It happens every four years, and it just happened again. That loud noise you heard was just the sound of a head-on collision as NBC's waning coverage of the 2012 Olympics ran smack into NBC's waxing coverage of the 2012 Elections, just prior to NBC's pending coverage of the 2014 Winter Olympics.

No bystanders were injured in the collision; fortunately, dozens of colored pie charts were killed.

Those sneaky Greeks and their sneaky every-four-year's games. Did they do this to us on purpose? Way back when, while they were thoughtlessly designing Olympic Games instead of going through Socrates' medicine cabinet and clearly marking the "poison" vials, do you think they knew? Did they foresee that, centuries later and continents away, another democracy would design every-four-year Presidential elections ... and then, like calendar masochists, schedule everything to happen during the same year?

205

In 776 BC, ancient naked people participated in the very first Olympic festival, which, according to the internet, was invented by Al Gore. The games were created to honor the gods and goddettes that inhabited Mount Olympus, which, according to MSNBC, was invented by Barack Obama. Like this year's event, those original games were also covered by NBC, back when they were still a tiny little start-up (Naked Broadcasting Citizen). And, like with our current Olympics, NBG had to deal with a bit of a time delay, while everybody sat around waiting for the famous emperor, Sid Caesar, to get born and invent the Orange Julius Calendar.

The first-ever ancient Olympics didn't go very well, due to the first-ever wardrobe malfunction. (you didn't really think all those Greek athletes were naked *on purpose*, do you?) But the second Olympic Games (Olympiad Deux) were rescued, thanks to the intervention of one Mittus Romnius, a self-starter from the outlying province of Mormos; a man who, like politicians, then and now, had a gift for managing armed naked guys. Contemporaries of Romnius called him a classic entrepreneur, which was a high compliment, given that nobody in BC had invented that word yet. Romnius also invented wind-proof hair.

Historical Sidebar: Generally speaking, that Mount Olympus crowd were just a bunch of loud, vindictive, pouty, pampered whiners, with access to insane amounts of power coupled with zero amounts of accountability. (In other words, they were the BC version of the US Congress.) However, the Olympians did possess one enviable characteristic: they were completely fictitious, which is a delicious concept indeed, especially when you consider the US Congress.

You Gonna Finish That Dragon?

If you watched the tail end of NBC's 2012 Olympics coverage, it was easy to tell that the Games were wrapping up, because NBC's crew were desperately scrabbling for airtime filler that they could shove in-between the few remaining, less-popular events. NBC producers were frantically slapping together James Bond retrospectives, re-scoring World War II mini-documentaries, or analyzing the deep-set theatrical motivations underlying some of the character choices made by Benny Hill and Mr. Bean.

At one point, NBC went so far as to provide live coverage of Tom Brokaw making anagrams from British-y words, like *Parliament*, *Lord Mountbatten-Smythe*, and *body English*.

But all that remained for NBC, Olympic-wise, was to cover those "niche" sports that don't require stadiums (or, to use the classical Greek plural for stadiums, *angora*).

And these last-day add-on sports are just not in the same popularity class as those timeless, "classic" Olympian crowd-swellers like track & field, swimming, soccer, and Mob Syndicate Badminton Wagering. No, these are the odd cousins; the red-headed step-sports. These are those back-page-of-the-program events that somehow, over the years, managed to sneak their way on to the Olympic schedule next to the "serious" athletic challenges, like running with a little stick, jumping over a high stick, and throwing a pointy stick. You know the ones:

- Solo Rhythmic Gymnastics: This sport usually features a tiny female from a country named Belalugosia, dressed like one of the background singers at an Elton John concert, and sporting enough mascara to forge a fake visa for Tammy Faye Bakker. For three minutes or so, she repeatedly dislocates all of her joints, on demand, while waving a long pastel-colored streamer. After she completes her routine, she hops up and down, the mascara waves madly at the audience, and then both collapse into racking sobs. As one might.

- Team Rhythmic Gymnastics: Here, we introduce Sir Elton's full "Rocket Man" chorus, and add hula hoops. For the allotted time, the participants rhythmically gymnasticate in such perfect synchronicity that you would swear they were actually computer-generated Belalugosians. And they do it all in time to abnormally unusual music. (I don't know who selects this music; let's just say that I wouldn't want to see that person standing outside my window in a fading twilight.) And then sometimes, just to make a change, the gymnasts will lob what look like giant red Q-tips at the ceiling. As one might.

- Full-Contact Speed Monopoly: Actually, I made this one up. But given some of the other stuff going on in the modern Olympics, I had to *tell* you I made it up, didn't I?

- Dressage: Here's one that doesn't even require an athlete at all. Now, I'm not saying horse riding has no value, in the grand scheme of things. I just don't grasp the Olympic athletic value of watching horses jump over fake fences while being ridden by perky pony-tailed Posture Pals dressed like Cracker Barrel gift shop lawn jockeys.

You Gonna Finish That Dragon?

But all weird things must come to an end - even Hunter Thompson-level weird things, like a major television network trying to pretend, in prime time, that its reruns of the Olympic Games aren't reruns of the Olympic Games.

And so, now, NBC News must prepare to fly home, switch theme songs, huddle with their counterparts at MSNBC, and gear up for their analysis of the 2012 Presidential Election (quickly, though, before the 2014 Winter Games!)

Are they up to the task of covering a Presidential election with respect, with intelligence, and without pointy sticks? I'll leave you with this defining Olympic moment, and let you be the judge.

In what is sure to secure them a Pulitzer Prize for investigative journalism, those hard news hawks at NBC broke this momentous sports story in the closing days of the 2012 Games: 16% of Olympic gold medal winners cry during the presentation of their medals. NBC analysts were also able to confirm that British athletes are the most likely to tear up, while athletes from China cry less than any other.

Ooh. Take that, Woodward and Bernstein.

Mary Had a Little Clam

How America nearly killed its own holiday
<>~<>~~~~~~~~~<>~<>~~~~~~~~~~<>~<>

Thanksgiving in America

As every schoolchild knows, unless they're overmedicated, Thanksgiving is a uniquely American holiday, along with our perennial President's Day White Sale, and the wildly popular The Post Office Lost Another Billion Dollars This Month Month.

Yes, Thanksgiving is a special time when we celebrate (among other things) our independence from Great Britain, a country defined by an untouchable caste of self-serving lawgivers, shrinking exports, and socialized medicine, all in the hands of a haughty, seemingly infallible royalty playing coddle-master to a whiny, uninformed electorate.

No, wait, that's *America*. Okay, never mind. Let's move on.

The First Thanksgiving

As most schoolchildren could tell you, if they weren't busy texting, the tradition now known as Thanksgiving began in the fall of 1621, when Pilgrims and Native Americans gathered together to celebrate a successful harvest (literal translation: "well, they're obviously not leaving, so let's create a White Sale"). On a whim, the Pilgrims decided to have a three-day feast, as opposed to their traditional methods of celebrating the arrival of winter (freezing and starving to death). They were joined by 108% of the local Wampanoag tribe. (*head count provided by the Plymouth Bipartisan Board of Poll Watchers*)

For that first Thanksgiving, the Wampanoag delegation was led by their tribal leader, Chief Ted 'Massasoit' Kennedy, who introduced the Pilgrim settlers to a vital food source ('maize') and introduced the Wampanoag to a vital revenue source ('maize tax'). Things went swimmingly until another member of the tribe, Deputy Assistant Under-Chief Willard 'Mittasoit' Romney, suggested the Pilgrims pay for the tribe's universal health care (literal translation: 'tax maze'). The plan didn't go over very well, there in pre-colonial Cape Cod, so Chief Willard was forced to move to Utah, where he founded Mormonism. That didn't go over very well, either, so in 1624, Romney moved to Iowa and began his long-standing tradition of running for President, once somebody invented the State Fair.

Overall, however, the first Thanksgiving feast represented a treasured moment in American history, since nobody yet had invented carbs, trans-fats, or PETA. According to the logs of Edward Winslow, a Pilgrim spokes-puritan, host and guest alike enjoyed a meal of deer, turkey and other fowl, clams and fish, berries, plums, and not boiled pumpkin. (Oh, they ate the boiled pumpkin. They just didn't enjoy it.)

And of course, after the first Thanksgiving, all the women went outside to wash dishes, hang the leftovers from a tree branch, and wait for somebody to invent Brad Pitt; meanwhile, the Pilgrim men passed out in primitive Lazy-Boys, waited for the Detroit game, and helped coin the word '*eructation*.' (a Latin term, loosely translated as '*pull my finger*')

Scattered Thanksgivings

Though we base our current Thanksgiving holiday on that first three-day grocery binge in 1621, it was hardly an overnight sensation. There were sporadic, regional celebrations, usually to give thanks for local events, such as the end of a drought, or the latest catalog of non-wooden teeth. But over 150 years went by before men from all thirteen colonies collectively celebrated a 'day of Thanksgiving,' after the guys spotted Dolly Madison in a bathing suit. (The women were still outside by the 'leftovers' tree, hacking at some frozen clams.)

In 1789, President George "Who's Ya Father?" Washington proclaimed Thursday, 26 November, as the very first national day of Thanksgiving. This was to be a day to celebrate the official formation of a new nation, so that America could officially begin borrowing billions of dollars from China. Unfortunately, though, the nation got sidetracked. Somebody invented the ACLU, and suddenly, all over the colonies, constitutional lawyers were having heated debates over odd, arcane things called 'clauses' and 'nuances' and 'per diem fees.' Then somebody pointed out that we didn't actually *have* a

Constitution yet, so everybody had to stop what they were doing and go draft one.

And so, even after a national day of Thanksgiving was declared in 1789, there was still no annual celebration.

Except for the lawyers.

The Mother of Thanksgiving

As it so often turns out, it took a woman to get the job done. We owe our modern Thanksgiving to Sarah Josepha Hale, a contemporary of President Lincoln who spent forty years of her life advocating for a national, annual Thanksgiving holiday. (Rumor has it that Sarah may have invested heavily in cranberries, but she's allowed to do that. It's in the Constitution. Look it up.)

Sarah Hale, by the way, was the editor of something called Godey's Lady's Book, and if that little factoid ever comes in handy, please let me know. But she's also credited as the author of the famous nursery rhyme, '*Mary Had a Little Lamb*,' a sad, irritating story about an underage stalker disguised as an albino farm animal. ('*And everywhere that Mary went...*')

And so, for forty long years, Sarah kept at it, year after year, endlessly demanding a Thanksgiving holiday, carping about cranberries, and reciting her famous poem at anyone who didn't see her coming. Finally, President Lincoln, who was willing to try just about anything ~~to shut her up~~ to hold America together, agreed to the idea, and on 3 October, 1863, he issued his Thanksgiving Proclamation, which declared the last Thursday in each November to be a day of thanksgiving and praise, and to signal the outbreak of holiday shopping.

Honest Abe christened the new Post Office holiday during a press conference in the Rose Garden, where he established another annual Thanksgiving tradition by pardoning two attorneys. In a spirit of bipartisanship, Congress adjourned until 1901.

FDR Bungs It Up

For the next 75 years, America got itself used to its annual, end-of-November Thanksgiving weekend. But then, in 1939, things changed again, thanks to President Franklin "Fear Itself" Roosevelt, a man who seemed to think the United States was his own personal box of Legos. Roosevelt, who was elected President so many times that the Republicans had to buy a new elephant, decided to just issue his own Thanksgiving Proclamation, thank you very much.

In 1939, FDR decided to yank Thanksgiving back a week, a bold, selfless move based on Roosevelt's deeply-held religious conviction that moving the holiday would extend the Christmas shopping season. Of course, the immediate result was mass confusion: calendars were now incorrect; school schedules were disrupted; Howard Cosell missed a connecting flight.

And then Americans did what Americans do. We made it worse.

The Schism

All across America, an uproar roared up, led by governors, politicians, and other life forms that depend on a host organism. Twenty-three States actually ignored the proclamation and kept right on being humble and thankful on the last weekend of the month. Twenty-three other States sided with FDR's new third-week Thanksgiving, while Colorado and Texas decided to celebrate both dates. In a spirit of bipartisanship, Congress just took the whole month off.

(This was back when we only had 48 States, as opposed to our current crop of 57.)

And so, there we were, a nation mired in quag. The holiday that had been established by President Lincoln to bring the country together was now doing the exact opposite - that other thing, that whaddayacallit thing that involves a bunch of rending, where stuff gets asundered.

Where would it all lead?

<drum roll>

Congress Fixes Everything

<rim shot>

You're right. That was its own joke.

Happy Thanksgiving!

The Midnight Ride of Paul Revere, DDS

The importance of July 4th. No, 2nd. No, wait...6th. No, wait...

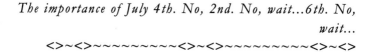

I wonder if, some 230-plus years ago, our founders and framers proudly signed their names, stood and shook hands all round, and thought, "Well met, patriots. One day, all across our new country, citizens will celebrate this great experiment, this thing called 'American independence,' with deep discounts on pickup trucks."

Obviously, the founders couldn't foresee the civilization...such as it is...that we live in today. They were grateful to get mail, monthly, from a guy on a horse; we whine when the internet is slow. They wore knickers - pants pulled up to their knees; we wear ours pulled right back down. They built their own houses, grew their own food, filled in as their own politicians; nowadays, we just buy all those things.

They had Poor Richard's Almanac. We have Grumpy Cat.

To be fair to the founders, however, we're hardly experts ourselves, on our own American history - *and we have it all written down.* As a nation, we are frightfully ignorant about our nation. Heck, our own President claims to have visited all 57 of our 50 states. What was he thinking? Studio 57? Heinz 57?

(I bet the founders never saw *that* coming, either. Whoa. You gotta wonder about a leader who confuses his own country with a steak sauce.)

Part of the problem, though, is the history books themselves. Witness:

- They're giant, cloth-bound tomes with titles like "The Stillbirth of a Nation" and "Federalist Nano-Tendencies In The Scourging of Mesoamerican Buffalo Mating Rituals, Vol. V"
- They're all written by people named Eldridge, or Alistair, or Something Something With Six Initials, like O.D.M. Prolestackage, PhD MBA LOL. Next time you're in the library, check out the US History section: not a Tommy or Katie in the whole card catalog.
- Each chapter ends in that most annoying of literary pastimes: Discussion Questions - a treat that serious literary efforts have managed to do without since, oh, Moses.

So, as we, the collective citizens of all 57 American states draw near to another annual day of celebration, let's review some of our shared history, the history that helped get us here. (No, Bobby, this will *not* be on the exam.)

>> The 1600s

As every schoolchild knows - even Bobby - America is a nation founded by Pilgrims, a group who left England in protest: they were a people of deep convictions, and thought it was wrong that Protestants had to buy hot dogs in packs of ten, but buns in packs of twelve. So the Pilgrims rented a moving van from Mayflower and sailed the thing to America, which came back to haunt them at "refundable deposit" time.

(The Pilgrims' progress was documented by the famous author, Paul Bunyan.)

In 1620, the Pilgrims beached their van in present-day Cape Cod, thereby becoming both America's first illegal immigrants *and* first under-dressed tourists. Shortly after embarking at Thirty Plymouth Rock, they were immediately shepherded into an ACORN office, where they signed pre-populated voter registration docs, were given free health care and in-state college tuition by the Obama administration, and offered a taxpayer-funded sex change, or an abortion, or both.

Having arrived safely in America, the Pilgrims eagerly embraced the local customs, like disappearing and starving to death. After that eagerness wore off, the surviving Pilgrims set up a limited liability corporation in Delaware and rebranded themselves as the Puritans. The colony couldn't escape the grip of their faraway British rulers, however, who insisted the Puritans burn witches in packs of eight, but buy stakes in bundles of six.

For the next few years, anti-British sentiment settled to a simmer, thanks to enterprising Americans: Samuel Adams invented the microbrewery (beer), and Ben Franklin invented electricity (*cold* beer). But England wouldn't back off, and tensions, um, tensed. Then, suddenly, we were having to invent new war-related words; words like foment, skirmish, and Bob Hope.

>> 1775

Fed up with foreign rule, several New England patriots set up The Revolutionary War (a limited liability corporation in Delaware). The fledgling war's first press release ("two if by sea") was delivered by a dentist-silversmith named Paul Revere, a mildly disturbed gentleman who'd somehow managed to convince himself that England - a country on the other side of the Atlantic Ocean - might figure out a way to attack America by land.

Contrary to legend, Dr. Revere did not gallop madly about New England yelling "The British are coming!" After all, most of the people in New England *were* British. That would be like you running around South Florida, warning people to be on the lookout for Jews in golf carts.

(Revere did, however, irritate several prominent Bostonians with his endless insistence that they floss.)

>> 1776

Anti-British tensions continued to foment and skirmish; some colonists even held mock funerals for England's King George III (pronounced *"George Ai Yi Yi"*).

The Declaration of Independence was signed on the Fourth of July...probably...although it could've been July 2nd, or August 2nd, or 6th. Founder John Adams stubbornly clung to the 2 July date; so stubbornly, in fact, that for years he refused to attend celebrations on the Fourth of July. According to insider sources, however, Adams was just being petty: sometime earlier, Adams' wife, Abigail, had come up with a line of sugary snack cakes, only to have the idea stolen by James Madison's wife, Little Debbie.

On the sixth of July, the Declaration of Independence was published for the first time, in the Pennsylvania Evening Post. Not yet appreciating the document's historical importance, however, the Post stubbed it in on page six, in-between "obits & witch burnings" and the Jumble.

The Second Continental Congress convened, created the Fourth of July holiday, and immediately adjourned for a two-week Fourth of July holiday, returning just in time to adjourn for the August recess.

>> 1777

The first formalized commemoration of American Independence was held in Philadelphia, that landmark-laced metropolis known far and wide as the City of Brotherly Love Unless You're In A Gang That My Gang's At War With.

>> 1778

To celebrate the country's Independence, General George Washington issued a double ration of rum to all his soldiers. Seizing the opportunity, fraternities at the University of

Virginia immediately declared two Independence Days per weekend during football season.

>> 1779

In 1779, the Fourth of July fell on a Sunday, so Americans postponed celebrating their Independence until July Fifth. (this was back before God was outlawed in the US)

An exception to the rescheduling was made for the frat houses at the University of Virginia, who patriotically honored (double rummy) both days. And the sixth. And the seventh through the fourteenth.

>> 1781

Massachusetts became the first of our 57 states to make the Fourth of July an official state holiday. Dentist Paul Revere became the first to officially prostitute the holiday, taking out a full-page ad offering deep discounts on deep cleaning.

>> 1791

The phrase "Independence Day" was coined by a travelling flag salesman, Thaddeus Independence. Merchandising included tiny flags emblazoned with 57 stars, Will Smith action figures, and a Jeff Goldblum bobble-head.

>> 1826

Exactly fifty years after the signing of the Declaration of Independence, both John Adams *and* Thomas Jefferson died on the Fourth of July; for years, however, Adams insisted he'd died two days earlier.

>> 1870

Congress made Independence Day a holiday for all federal employees. (In 1870, there were only about fourteen federal employees.)

But something about the holiday didn't feel right.

>> 1941

Ah. There it is. Congress made Independence Day a *paid* holiday for all federal employees.

All 57 million of 'em.

~-~-~-~-~-~

Well, wasn't *that* uplifting! (the true parts, anyway) Don't you feel patriotic now? Bet you didn't know Paul Revere was a dentist, did you? Hmm?

Now, get out there and celebrate your American heritage. Be a patriot - buy a truck. Heck, buy 57 trucks - one from each state. And don't forget to floss.

Otherwise, the terrorists win.

National Really Large Italian Month

For far too long, Halloween has hogged October. Enough already.

<>~<>~~~~~~~~~<>~<>~~~~~~~~~~<>~<>

I really hope you didn't get distracted and miss it, but it's my job to get the word out: 24 October was National Bologna Day.

I know, I know. Lots of people didn't. But try to be strong. Take a minute to pull yourself together, if you need. But I'll bet that, next year, you'll be paying a little more attention to these things, won't you? Mmm?

National Bologna Day - that one day a year when we celebrate the career of actor Joseph Bologna.

No, I made that up. National Bologna Day is a day set aside to pay our respects to Baloney, a city in northern Italy known as the birthplace of Oscar Mayer, the first Earl of Sandwich.

I made that up, too. Starting to see a pattern yet?

If you think about it, and I doubt you will, and I don't blame you, it's hard to grasp the monumental coincidence necessary that would allow a National Bologna Day to fall this close to a Presidential Election Day.

On the other hand, it makes perfect sense. I mean, for direct-dialed, high-impact baloney, you just can't beat a Joe Biden stump speech. At any minute during any speech, you half-expect his ears to spout mustard, forcing Congress to grab a frying pan, subsidize white bread, and declare a National Fried Sandwich Day, or at least name a Post Office after Joseph Bologna.

As it turns out, the month of October is just jam-packed with holidays, though you rarely hear about most of them unless you're a member of Congress, in which case you're preparing to not work during any of them; after all, you just returned from not working during any of September's holidays. (Not working is what Congress calls 'recess.' And when you think about that arrogant asylum of warring brats, 'recess' is the perfect word for it.)

Every single day in October plays host to at least one holiday. For example, 10 October is 'World Mental Health Day,' which we usually celebrate by yelling at people in traffic. But 11 October - *the very next day* - is 'Take Your Teddy Bear to Work Day.' And it's bizarre scheduling like this, I think you'll agree, that helps explain how October got its nickname: 'National Sarcasm Awareness Month.'

(Coincidentally, 15 October is 'National Grouch Day.' I guess HR finally made your boss get rid of his teddy bear.)

Obviously, though, when it comes to holidays in October, National Bologna Day doesn't get a lot of attention, unless you're Joseph Bologna, or a devotee of the Pork Channel (not to be confused with C-SPAN). But neither do many other very fine October holidays. Witness:

- National Mole Day *(not to be confused with Take Your Ferret to Work Day)*
- National Mule Day *(take a border-jumping drug runner to lunch!)*
- Count Your Buttons Day *(renamed in 1998 by Bill Clinton to 'Velcro Appreciation Day')*
- Increase Your Psychic Powers Day *(Yes, really. I am not good enough to make this stuff up.)*
- Reptile Awareness Day *(Actually, I think every day should be filled with reptile awareness. Personally, whenever I become Aware of a Reptile, I immediately respond by celebrating National Run Away Day, followed closely by Run Straight Into A Tree Day.)*

Contrary to what you might be thinking, National Mole Day is not a day to celebrate spies (see *'Drug Runners'*), nor garden pests (see *'Congress'*), nor is it the time to stare at that dark, disturbing hair-capped spot on your coworker's chin. National Mole Day is actually about chemistry. (I say that up front, in case you want to skip this part and go do something more interesting, like counting your buttons.)

See, in the world of career chemists, which is a cold and blisteringly dull place where sex appeal goes to die, a 'mole' is a basic measuring unit that equals the atomic mass of a single molecule. (Counting buttons yet?)

The actual number of a mole is 6.02 x 10^23, which is a number so large that mathematicians are forced to describe it to us 'civilians' by using emoticon-like symbols:

- 0 (buttons)
- X (kisses)
- ^ (single-family housing)

Thanks to their intervention, therefore, we non-scientific 'laymen' can now grasp the staggering size of this mole whaddayacallit thingie. A mole is, like, really huge and stuff.

A monstrous number. In fact, if Congress were to take one recess for every mole zero, I wouldn't be a bit surprised.

Anyway, it's that mole's number that we now celebrate on National Mole Day, a number known to mathematicians and chemists who hang out in General Sciences Karaoke Bars as "Avogadro's Number," since it was discovered by an Italian named Amadeo Avogadro's Number.

According to the internet, Avogadro's full name was Lorenzo Romano Amadeo Carlo Avogadro, conte de Quaregna e di Cerreto (literal translation: 'Oscar Meyer'). But his parents couldn't afford to embroider all that on his lunchbox, so they just went with Amadeo (literal translation: 'a movie about Mozart').

You Gonna Finish That Dragon?

Legend has it that Avogadro challenged chemistry's conventional wisdom (that kind of picky 'can't leave well enough alone' nonsense went on all the time in the 1800s). Chemists at the time depended heavily on a construct known as the Law of Definite Proportions, but around 1810, Avogadro met Sophia Loren, had an epiphany (literal translation: 'misdemeanor'), and came up with the Law of Multiple Proportions. And the rest was, as they say, baloney.

No, in the "Everybody's Favorite Holiday" contest, Baloney Day and its mates don't stand a chance. And why is that?

You know why.

This annual slighting of what would otherwise be perfectly good festive days is due to the looming presence of that overpowering holiday monolith that steals October's spotlight - yes, you know the one I'm talking about:

Four Prunes Day.

No, I'm talking of course about that autumnal crowd-pleaser, Halloween, that magical late-October evening when, all across America, eager children, many of them old enough to default on a mortgage, dress up in costumes, fearlessly trespass, and extort candy from homeowners who actually *are* defaulting on a mortgage, all to celebrate an ancient mystery: the official kick-off of the Christmas shopping season.

By the way, if you're looking for ways to fully immerse yourself in 'Increase Your Psychic Powers Day' ... and who isn't? ... here are some suggestions from a particularly lame, lashed-together, holiday-focused website, one of those cloyingly cute, exclamation-point-laced e-efforts that refuse to be shackled by outdated concepts like spelling, grammar, and punctuation:

- Get out the Ouija board! Use it with some friends! *(Do this repeatedly until you don't have any friends left. It won't take long.)*
- Flip a coin and guess heads or tails. Over time, as your psychic power increases, you should guess correctly more than 50% of the time. *(Also, over time, people will stop inviting you to go places, and coworkers will start leaving Thorazine brochures on your desk.)*
- When the phone rings, guess who it will be. As you go through the day, guess what people are going to say. *(As your psychic power increases, accost random strangers in the grocery, spin them around, and yell, "I know! I know!")*
- Get out a deck of cards. Shuffle them well. Think of what the top card is. Then, turn it over. *(Better yet, don't even bother turning it over. Just tell people you're psychic. Tell everyone you meet. Say it loudly, while wearing various hats. Don't forget to update your résumé!)*

One final note: I'm told that, somewhere in the October calendar, there's an International Skeptics Day.

I'm not buying it.

Seasonal Affective Disorder Defection

Going out like a lamb? I think not.

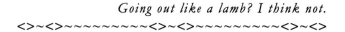

As one grows older, new things begin to weigh on one's mind. I suppose that's one of the inevitabilities of becoming a mature adult, like living with eyebrow dandruff, or hoping that somebody who used to give you wedgies in Junior High School gets indicted for a major crime and has to spend his golden years in a dank, poorly-ventilated penal facility "making new friends."

Pondering such thoughts is as unavoidable as the thoughts themselves, and as unavoidably disturbing. For example: what is the point, the life-enhancing benefit, of eyebrow dandruff? Frankly, I'm missing it. And other thoughts bubble up: must one *really* be warned that, after a package spends 45 minutes in a 400-degree oven, its "contents may be hot?" If one wants to say the word "slut" in the news media, does one have to donate a million bucks to a presidential re-election campaign? And at what age, exactly, does one get so stuffy and stodgy that one starts referring to oneself as "one?"

Real posers, these, especially for someone like me, whose idea of a wild week is to buy more than three ripe bananas ... *at the same time.* But with the passage of time, I've also modulated socially and politically. Values shift, priorities adjust. And so, I've come to a decision, and I want to share that decision with all of you. I've decided to become a Liberal.

I think it all began when I was watching the news, and it just hit me. Liberals have learned a new debating tactic, and I *like* it. When confronted by "the other side" with pesky details, like, say, facts, Liberals have figured it out -- just shake your head back and forth, slowly, with a pitying half-smile. I *like* it. You can practically hear the subtext: "Tsk, tsk. Ah, these poor, stupid people who don't agree with me. Good thing I'm here to manage their lives. Oops! Aw, that's okay - let him get up by himself." I *like* that. Any defense can be flattened if hit by enough condescension bombs.

Liberals, it seems, have an edge in our political discourse. They may not be winning the war, but they seem to be winning all the battles. And they've added a new twist to their rock-solid logic: repetition. Whatever their stance on whatever issue, they just parrot it over and over and over until, like some fake rock exposed to clever medieval alchemy, it becomes true. These days, what wins the day is not what's *reported* - it's what's *repeated*. Also, Liberals will blame anybody (else) for anything. And Republicans are too busy blaming each other to duck. Liberals counsel, "We'll take care of you because you're really stupid, but that's not your fault." Republicans counter with, "Look, we *know* we're not the solution, so re-elect us and we'll fight for term limits."

For you stubbornly neurotic black helicopter-ites out there who will want to somehow shoehorn racial issues into my defection decision, please allow me to counter with this indestructible Aristotelian bulwark: Shut up.

Often, far too often, a point that gets missed by cerebral flatliners, raw-meat-gnawing knuckle-walkers, and other MSNBC anchors, is this: a person - regardless of political persuasion or ideological bent - *can* sometimes disagree with someone else, and it's *not* because that someone else has more (or less) melanin. It's because that someone else is a moron. Racism is stupid, yes. But stupidity can be color-blind. But let's move on - we could spend weeks just talking about stupid. Why, MSNBC alone...

Of course, my defection is going to mean that I may alienate friends, family, and citizens of facebook. Well, maybe not facebook. To alienate facebookers, you need to announce your allegiance to much more horrid things, like books that don't have any pictures, or beef, or Christianity. (To fall out of favor at facebook, you need to commit some virtual faux pas in Farmville or Frontierville, like trying to hoard magic baby carrots *before* unlocking the non-rideable Bicycle Coupon that unleashes the Button Dwarf by picking twelve repeatable Blue Ribbon Mafia missions all at once instead of four at a time. Pfft. As if.) Here: here's an anecdote from my past will give you an idea of what I may be up against -- once, while was I was at university, my girlfriend jokingly mentioned to her family that she'd be home for Thanksgiving, and bringing a guest: a transsexual Somali Liberal Rastafarian ex-con who was a practicing cannibal, had eleven fingers and no ears, and was born with kneecaps in the place where people usually have eyebrows. Her family was aghast: "Don't you *dare* bring home a Liberal."

Lastly, then, if you'll look back and take note of the first letter in each paragraph, you'll understand why I've come to this decision, and why I feel driven to share it with you. Please wish me well.

Casserole Belli

Leave it to humans to combine food and fighting
<>~<>~~~~~~~~~~<>~<>~~~~~~~~~~<>~<>

It was my fault. It was an unguarded moment.

Last week, you may have watched the annual Fourth of July hot dog-eating contest on TV. I caught a few moments of the event, because it was a holiday weekend, and because I wasn't fast enough to change the channel.

Guys, in obvious agony (of *course* it was guys), trying to inhale more *a la carte* hot dogs than *other* guys, before *any* of the guys got violently ill, or got disowned by their parents, or landed a supporting role in an Adam Sandler movie.

I'm not sure how best to describe it, but "inhumanly foul" is a strong candidate. "Bat-barking nasty" comes close, as does "Aztec Weekend at the frat house," but neither expression really roasts the Roget piglet. It was a lot like what I imagine life would be like on a planet inhabited by feral alien jackals, if feral alien jackals had caveman egos, wore sponsor t-shirts, and had Hooters Girls.

Personally, I have to reach *way* back to remember the last time I volunteered to participate in a televised group activity where one's manhood was measured by who didn't retch. (see "Aztec Weekend")

But whacky food competitions don't end at Coney Island. Point your car westward - you won't have to drive far to sample some more of America's high-impact low cuisine. For example, there's the Roadkill Cook-Off in Marlington, West Virginia, part of the area's theoretically popular Autumn Harvest Festival. (As if you needed any more reasons to come back to Marlington, West Virginia.)

Sadly, the culinary warriors of Marlington don't use real, tire tread-treated roadkill. (Our dedication to responsible journalism demands that we let you know that.) Rather, they just cook things that often *become* roadkill: possum, deer, characters in Stephen King novels, very small trucks. One year's winning recipe was "Pulled Bambito under Saboogo." And you know how hard it can be to find good saboogo.

Next stop? Clinton, Montana.

Its politically correct name is the Rocky Mountain Oyster Festival. (Our dedication to family-friendly journalism prevents us from provided a more anatomically correct description of this contest's entrée. Let's just say that the ranches around Clinton, Montana are home to some very paranoid bulls. On the other hand, the local church choir has a fabulous soprano section.) You can order your 'oysters' deep-fried, beer-battered, or marinated. There's also a $5 sampler plate, a common favorite among the type of female that Shakespeare might refer to as a "shrew." This popular, late-summer event has a motto, too. And no, I'm not going to.

On to Arizona.

Years ago, the town of Yuma slept late on City Slogan Day, and that's why they're now known as "The Winter Lettuce Capital of the World." So it was just a matter of time before somebody thought up the annual Yuma Lettuce Days. Book your trip early: you don't want to miss the Lettuce Sculptures, full-contact Cabbage Bowling, and the uncomfortably named "Toss It Up" Salad Bar.

The Gilroy Garlic Festival, held in Garlic, California, is sponsored by Altoids. No, it isn't. (Our dedication to responsible journalism just barely won out on that one.) Each July, some 100,000 halitosis-deprived visitors descend upon Gilroy to eat garlic-based recipes, listen to garlic-oriented music, and congratulate the year's Garlic Queen, all in a designated vampire-free zone. The collective guests will consume 2.5 tons of garlic during the three-day event, and you haven't lived till you've seen 100,000 people simultaneously positioning to stand upwind of each other.

In the spring, be sure to consider the Waikiki Spam Jam. For one glorious day in April, you can try something called *Spam Musubi*, which I'm told is like sushi, except instead of ingesting undercooked, parasite-laden fish, you get Spam.

Tough call.

And though we've barely scratched the stove surface of America's vittle violence, let's not forget our international brothers and sisters! After all, other countries can be just as stupid as us. (Um...as stupid as we. *Are.* As we *are.* Um...more stupider than even ourselves, even. Us our own selves. Um...)

The Ivrea Orange Festival in Italy dates back to the 12th Century, when girls would stand on balconies and wing oranges at guys they liked. (Actual sex wasn't invented until the 13th Century, right after somebody invented the balcony ladder.) The guys then started tossing oranges back at the girls, until fascism was invented to get things under control.

And now, in keeping with our fresh produce motif, let's duck over to Bunol, a town in the Valencia region of Spain, for the *La Tomantina* festival. ("Valencia," from the ancient Moors, meaning "naval orange") Every year, during the last weekend of August, 9,000 locals and some 40,000 obviously bored visitors descend on the town square to throw tomatoes at each other. Why? Well, in honor of the Virgin Mary, of course. Duh. Obviously, *you're* not Spanish.

Actually, the tomato wars are the wrap-up: the third act. The festival opens with a person attempting to scale a greased pole to capture a cooked ham (we're a bit unclear as to the underlying theology). Once the ham has been subdued and has promised to behave, water cannons are trained on everybody in the square, much to the amusement of the ham. What happens next is exactly what you, as a student of European history, would expect: over 100 tons of tomatoes are dumped out into the streets, in a frenzied, semi-holy kind of way.

You Gonna Finish That Dragon?

And then the tomato tossing begins. As the Virgin Mother would have wished.

Spain also brings us a *goat* tossing festival - it takes place in Manganeses de la Polvorosa. Here's how *that* works: in order to honor *their* town's patron saint, some guy finds a goat (don't even go there), ties up the goat, carries the bound beast up to the church belfry, and then ... well, it *is* called a goat tossing festival, isn't it.

Now, before the pro-goat PETA hate mail starts pouring in, please understand that this is *not* some kind of coordinated goat sacrifice. At least, not intentionally. The plan is for the villagers who are standing below the belfry to catch the goat, in a tarpaulin that hopefully somebody didn't forget to bring. It's not like the Polvorosans are having a rousing game of goat badminton or something. But, since PETA may already be suited up, let's move on to Germany, home of...

The Goose Clubbing Festival.

Not much else I need to add here.

But I will say this: due to a medieval avalanche of animal rights' complaints, the Germans *did* agree to start using a goose that was already dead.

Not to be outdone, Spaniards once held a gay little festival that revolved around a man hanging from an (also pre-dead) goose until very disturbing things, anatomically speaking, happened to the ex-goose.

And here's one more from Spain. In Vilanova i La Geltru, Fat Tuesday begins with the Meringue Wars - yes, you guessed it: local children rush to the local bakeries, who hand out pies as ammunition. Shortly thereafter, as the adults sober up and join in, some 200,000 pounds of pies, cereal and candy go airborne.

It is seismic-level fun for everyone, and it singlehandedly helped revive Spain's struggling dental implant industry.

At the end of the day, the civic spectacular ends in the obvious way: the ceremonial burial of a sardine.

And all of this - pie artillery, dental issues, and sardine funerals - to mark the beginning of ... what else? ... Lent.

That, you have to admit, is a really special level of psychosis. Spain, apparently, is Europe's answer to Florida.

And speaking of Fat Tuesday, be sure to budget for a trip to Olney, England, for the next Olney Pancake Race! Every year, at 11.55am on that special day, the local ladies line up at the starting line, dressed in traditional housewife attire and armed with a frying pan that contains one pancake.

And yet, still, some will say there's no passion in Britain.

The race begins. The Olney mums have to flip the flapjack, run 415 yards through the greater metro Olney area, and then, at the finish line, toss the pancake once again. According to legend, this Benny-Hillian feat has been going on since 1445, which makes you wonder how bone-chillingly boring England must've been in 1444.

Of course, boring's not the worse thing that could happen. Things could always be worse. Just ask a German goose.

Barry Parham

Dude, Your Lang Syne is, like, Auld

Sneaking another year past the Mayan goalie

<>~<>~~~~~~~~~~<>~<>~~~~~~~~~~<>~<>

By the time some of you read this, we'll have begun a brand new year. And you know what *that* means: over ten whole workdays before government employees will get another paid holiday.

My goodness - the things those poor (un-) Civil (dis-) Service drones put up with.

But even for us bill-paying mortals, year's end heralds its *own* gauntlet of unavoidable traditions, doesn't it?

- The trick of figuring out where to store that vaguely-familiar fruitcake until next Christmas, when you can re-gift the nasty thing to whomever's next in the Holiday Fruitcake Circle of Life
- Preparing to spend somewhere between two and fifty-two weeks writing the wrong year on our personal checks

- New Year's Eve parties laced with over-dressed, under-medicated women, who spend the evening trying to fight off under-dressed, over-indulging guys, who spend the evening trying to impress the women by swilling shots of Jagermeister until they devolve into some kind of semi-simian extra from '*Altered States*'

- Another traffic snarl at the mall as millions of Americans try to return unwanted gifts - like monogrammed toilet seats or perfumes that smell like homeless yak saliva - even though they have no purchase receipts

- A clutch of college football bowl games, steeped in tradition, with traditional bowl game names; like the Unfinished Furniture Liquidators Bowl (played in the Midwestern Kansas Aluminum Siding Outlet stadium), brought to you by Big Tony's Toilet Emporium; or the Lowe's Employees Who Got Downsized But Found A Job Across The Street At Home Depot Bowl (sponsored by "Cleveland Soccer Moms Against Homeless Yak Cruelty")

- The annual announcement that this past year's Congress set a new record as the most useless, unproductive, and disliked Congress in history, at least until this next Congress gets a shot at the title

- Top Ten Lists

It's an unwritten law: Every old year must end with a new crop of Top Ten Lists. And every year, there are dozens of sources, compiling hundreds of Top Ten Lists cataloging thousands of categories: Top Ten Best Films, Top Ten Worst TV Shows,

Top Ten Larry King Divorces. Best-Dressed People, Best Worst-Dressed People, Best Nearly-Dressed People Appearing During Halftime at the Super Bowl. Top Ten Public Insults, Top Ten Private Apologies, Top Ten Tweets That Mention Either Vampires, Zombies, Or Mayans. Top Ten Christmas Gifts That Don't Contain Yak Products. Top Ten Reasons Why There Always Seems To Be A Lowe's Right Across The Street From A Home Depot.

Here are some actual lists that you can find on the internet, as far as you know:

Top Ten Annoying Christmas Songs
Topping the list again this year is "The Twelve Days of Christmas," followed closely by anything recorded by Burl Ives. Oddly enough, the other eight entries are all "Dominick, the Christmas Donkey."
Note: "Grandma Got Run Over by A Reindeer" got several Most Annoying votes, but the judges wisely opted to put that tune in its own category, feeling that it would be unfair to rank amateur irritants with pros like "Grandma..."

Top Ten Countries That Have Disappeared
This one was a bit of a tease. Here you'll find anti-climactic entries like East Germany, South Vietnam, and Detroit. For whatever reason, the list excluded land masses like Atlantis, Oz, and Rosanne Barr.

Top Ten Physical Ailments That Keep Hillary From Testifying
Sure, we gave her a pass on "stomach flu." Sure, the very next week, we let her slide on "I fell down." Yeah, we begrudgingly

gave her the benefit of the doubt when she announced "the heartbreak of psoriasis." But we believe the lady doth protest too much with this latest dodge: "I simply *can't* testify in these shoes." Stoppeth it. Shutteth up.

Top Ten Lame College Sports Nickname Changes
This year's winners include The Rainbow Warriors of the University of Hawaii, who dropped the "Rainbow" part thanks to a marketing decision, after desperate recruiters feared that "rainbows" had too many gay connotations. Sources say that a counter-suit has been filed by two well-known rainbow aficionados, Dorothy from Oz and Kermit the Frog, but we were unable to confirm those reports due to the case's pending status, and the fact that Dorothy and Kermit don't exist.
The Top Ten list also includes the Syracuse Orangemen, who are now simply the Syracuse Orange. College administrators cited a desire to become more gender-neutral, and "Syracuse Orangepersons" wouldn't fit on the faculty guest towels.

Top Ten Adam West Roles Other Than Batman (This is kinda sad. After all, three of the ten roles were Adam playing himself. Let's move on.)

Top Ten Hobbits You Didn't Know Existed
This is sad, too, because it means there are unsupervised people running around out there who think *any* hobbits actually exist. I hope nobody tells them about Kermit.

Top Ten Best Things About Windows 8
We got nothing. Anyone?

Top Ten Worst Regulations of 2012

You Gonna Finish That Dragon?

To those who compiled this list, we have to tip our hat; after all, it couldn't have been easy, picking only ten idiot maneuvers by Congress. Beyond the obvious mutton-headed moves, like daring each other to read ObamaCare, Congress focused this year on critical national security issues like Dishwasher Efficiency Standards and free Vatican-endorsed condom distribution.

But, in the spirit of the season, don't be too hard on lawmakers based solely on this past year. After all, legislators as a life form were idiots far before we flipped the ol' calendar page to January 2012.

In fact, once upon a time, overbearing lawmakers in one U.S. State passed a law that actually made it *illegal* for a river to rise above a certain level.

Whoa. Folks, that's some serious megalomania. Next thing you know, they'll be regulating toilet flushes, and banning large soft drinks.

Nah. That could never happen in America.

Marvin, Attorney to the Gods

How to live like there's no tomorrow, when there's a
tomorrow

<>~<>~~~~~~~~~<>~<>~~~~~~~~~~<>~<>

All right, this is getting ridiculous. Now they're telling us the predictions were wrong. Now, they're saying, the world will *not* end this year.

Probably.

Great. *Now* they tell me - and I just got my ObamaCare voucher for taxpayer-funded law school tuition, holistic cell-phone minutes, and free contraception.

But there it is. Based on the most recent 'analysis' of new 'data' discovered by 'guys with a grant' exploring what grant-granting experts refer to as 'a hole,' the Mayans were wrong about this December's pending Big Un-Bang. Or we were wrong about the Mayans. Or wrong about their calendar. Or we were looking in the wrong century. Or the wrong hole.

Probably.

C'mon, Science-Type People! Make up your minds! Those of us out here in real life, us non-tenured proles, we gotta make some plans, and get on with whatever's left of our lives! We have more, or possibly less, things to do! Do we replace the roof or just go with duct tape? Do we save that touted nine cents by opting for the cable/internet/phone bundle or not? Do we default on a 30-year fixed or do we default on an ARM? And what's the opposite of *default*? Fault?

But just in case they're wrong about being wrong:

Things Not To Buy If The World Is Ending

- Perennials
- Anything by Stephen King
- Bulk clothing, sold by the pound from Jos. A. Bank
- KGB-sized super-saver discount packs of Joe Biden pie-hole corks
- "Hillary in 2016" buttons
- Old pork or new cheese
- Will Call tickets to "The Lion King"
- Extended warranties (technically, not part of this list - I'm just saying)
- Obama's new book, "An Alphabetical List of My Accomplishments Prior to Adoption of the Gregorian Calendar, Part I"
- Facebook stock options, or casket futures

Ah, those madcap Mayans. Those doomsday stormcrows. Those nearly-naked tanned guys, with their deep-blue feather fetishes, those oddly-spelled nouns, that miserably misunderstood calendar, and a seriously proscriptive program for organ donors. The Mayans - the *original* purple people-eaters.

But new facts have emerged about the Mayans and their calendar, according to a paper published by The National Academy of Looking in Guatemalan Holes. While studying the Eighth-Century Mayan city known as Xultun (pronounced 'Boise'), scientists discovered an underground cave, as opposed, I suppose, to an above-ground cave. (Remember: these are people who received a federal grant.)

The scientists went into the cave (pronounced 'Qarlsbad Qaverns'), and painted on the cave's wall were some numbers and the words "Have you been injured?" (pronounced 'refrigerator magnet')

The scientists also noticed drawings of stacked bars and dots which they determined to be a calendar, because at lunch they'd gotten into the local beer. However, after a few more six-packs of discussion, they decided the bars and dots represented the story of basketball being introduced to Earthlings by rectangular space aliens (pronounced 'Dennis Rodman'). The next morning, however, the scientists returned to their original interpretation and began yelling about the world coming to an end on 21 December, and they kept yelling it until the cantinas agreed to reopen.

So let's review. Basically, we're supposed to believe that the world will end this year because somebody who was vetted by Congress found a number scratched into the wall of a damp cave.

I know, I know. It's hard to argue with such empirical evidence. So let's sweeten the pot. Here's some more hard science found in the chamber:

- The numbers on the cave wall were scratched *next to a mural of a man wearing a red crown and blue feathers.* (fortunately, italics had already been invented)
- Peeking out from behind that man was *another man.* (now debunked, in archeological circles, as a hoax known as 'The Peeking Man')
- A translated hieroglyphic warned, "Extended warranties are for suckers." (true then, true now)
- A calendar inscription pointed to a four-year interregnum (literal translation: 'acid reflux'), which was wrongly diagnosed as mesothelioma, resulting in a fatal outbreak of either lawyers or smallpox.

In the face of such an array of indisputable facts, you can see how the 21st Century's entire global scientific community might have gotten red herring-ed.

So here we were, ready to make not-so-long-term planet-wide plans, based on subterranean scrawls scribbled by a civilization that hadn't even finished inventing clothes, much less the full-court press or the downtown jump shot. We were ready to globally shut down shop because of a cave-wall chalk portrait of some blurry guy in an Elton John hat.

Imagine that fateful calendar-carving day in the cave of the King:

~~-~~-~~-~~

You Gonna Finish That Dragon?

Guard: Halt! State your business, puny-child-of-mortals.

Scribe: Can the theatrics, Marvin. It's me. Is the big guy in?

Marvin: Yeah, but he's eating Lunch.

Scribe: What do you mean, Lunch? Why the capital L?

Marvin: *Lunch* was the guy's name.

Scribe: Point taken.

Marvin: So how about that game last night, eh?

Scribe: We were robbed.

Marvin: Who knew Pizarro had cannons? They weren't listed in the lineup.

Scribe: I can't wait till somebody invents referees. So, can I go in and see Vault of Heaven's Imperial Jaguar And Immortal Chaser of Stars or what?

Marvin: Enter, lower-than-toad-toenail-fungus-discount-cleanser.

Scribe: Keep it up, Smallpox Boy. Keep it up.

Marvin: Your momma's a llama.

Scribe: Your Highness?

King: Ormum nmrlm?

Scribe: Got a minute, Mighty Sky Panther And Ultimate Shizzle?

King: Mzun NHM!

Marvin: Slowly, sir. Chew slowly. Remember the last time you had Mexican. And don't swig your marrow.

Scribe: Love your tan, sir. Not just anybody can pull that off, you know, living underground. Tres chic.

King: Well, hello, T'ah'ak T'u Oxicontn! Welcome, scribe! What brings you down here while I'm eating, a rash act that, depending on my mood, could result in me having you gutted like a Chilean sea bass and sliced into seventeen astrologically-favorable pieces?

Oxicontn: I wanted to wrap up that little calendar issue, if y...

King: Guard! Any heart left?

Marvin: Sure. Here you are, sir.

King: You were saying?

Oxicontn: The calendar, sir. That mathematician's here.

King: Oh, for Goxntotl's sake.

You Gonna Finish That Dragon?

Oxicontn: I know, I know. But you have to make a decision about the fourteenth Baktun before the rainy season; otherwise, in the distant future, Paul Theroux might write a novel. So if you'll jus...

King: You gonna finish those friars?

~~-~~-~~-~~

For now, though, the science people have canceled the calendar crisis. But just in case they're right about being wrong, here's a takeaway:

Books You Can Finish Before The World Ends

- The Collected Sonnets of Ozzy Osbourne
- "Women I Respect" by Bill Clinton
- Joy Behar's Fashion Tips
- "No, Really, We're Not!" (A Virtual Tour of Iran's Nuclear Centrifuges)
- Spicy Recipes From The English Countryside
- "Don't Pat Me, Bro!" - The Search for Dignity at US Airports
- Dr. Suess's Haiku Weekend

Keep that list in your pocket. At the very least, it'll get you through the next holiday season.

Probably.

<>~<>~~~~~~~~~~~<>~<>~~~~~~~~~~<>~<>

###

ABOUT THE AUTHOR

Barry Parham is a recovering software freelancer and the author of humor columns, essays and short stories. He is a music fanatic and a 1981 honors graduate of the University of Georgia.

Writing awards and recognitions earned by Parham include taking First Place in the November 2009 Writer's Circle Competition, First Prize in the March 2012 writing contest at HumorPress.com, and a plug by the official website of the Erma Bombeck Writers' Workshop. Most recently, Parham's work has appeared in three national humor anthologies.

Author's website
http://www.barryparham.com

@ facebook
http://www.facebook.com/pmWriter

@ Google+
http://tinyurl.com/n6w5gq4

@ Twitter
http://twitter.com/barryparham